Value for Money in the Public Sector

The Decision Maker's Guide

VALUE FOR MONEY IN THE PUBLIC SECTOR

The Decision Maker's Guide

Henry A. Butt and D. Robert Palmer

Basil Blackwell

© H. A. Butt and D. R. Palmer
Price Waterhouse, 1985

First published 1985

Basil Blackwell Ltd
108 Cowley Road, Oxford OX4 1JF, UK

Basil Blackwell Inc.
Suite 1505, 432 Park Avenue South,
New York, NY 10016, USA

British Library Cataloguing in Publication Data

Butt, Henry A.
    Value for money: a guide to principles and
    good practice in the public sector.
    1. Great Britain—Appropriations and expenditures
    I. Title   II. Palmer, D. Robert
336.3'9'0941   HJ2097

ISBN 0-631-14452-8
ISBN 0-631-14453-6 Pbk

Library of Congress Cataloguing in Publication Data

Butt, Henry A.
    Value for money

    Bibliography: p.
    Includes index.
    1. Finance, Public. 2. Management by objectives.
3. Program budgeting. 4. Management audit. I. Palmer.
D. Robert. II. Title
HJ131.B88   1985   350.72'22   85-6141
ISBN 0-631-14452-8
ISBN 0-631-14453-6 (pbk.)

Typeset by Getset (BTS) Ltd, Eynsham, Oxford
Printed in Great Britain by Billing and Sons Ltd, Worcester

Contents

Preface

During the course of writing the Price Waterhouse Value for Money Auditing Manual, we visited the United States, Canada and a number of other countries. One of the purposes of these visits was to investigate the range of books and other literature available on the subject of achieving better value for money in the public sector. We found that a large amount of material is available but that much of it, while excellent, is theoretical and nearly all of it appears to be written for the technician or practitioner. We could find little that we would recommend as a practical guide to a politician or a senior officer in the public sector, such as a head of department. We had in mind those who wished to gain an appreciation of the current state of development of value for money techniques and of how to implement an effective value for money regime but who would not be directly involved in its day to day operation. We have written this book to fill the gap we identified.

This English volume is the first in a series which is being published in each of the main European languages on this subject. We intend it to be a further instalment in the contribution Price Waterhouse is making internationally to the development of techniques and procedures for achieving better value for money for taxpayers.

Henry Butt and Bob Palmer

Acknowledgements

The authors record their thanks for the considerable help, encouragement and support they have received from colleagues in and associated with Price Waterhouse. Particular thanks are due to John Glynn of Exeter University for preparing Chapters 2 and 10, to Colin Sutherland of Price Waterhouse Europe for preparing material for Chapter 4 and other research and to Mick Archer MBE of Pedmore for preparing the index. We are grateful to Joan Thorneycroft for typing innumerable drafts, Clive Sadler for a constant flow of advice and comment and to Dr John Blackburn MP and Councillor Jack Edmonds OBE.

Value for Money ACTION Plan

	Chapter
Total commitment by senior elected representatives and officials. Right attitude to achieving VFM should permeate whole organisation.	▷ **3**
Small, powerful but representative committee to direct and co-ordinate VFM projects. Corporate approach to VFM should be adopted.	▷ **3**
Clearly defined strategic and operational objectives and targets for all functions and activities.	▷ **3**
Officials trained in management as well as technical matters.	▷ **3**
Key performance measures used for all major functions to evaluate and monitor productivity and effectiveness.	▷ **4**
Performance measures linked to performance targets for operational management so that productivity gains achieved during VFM reviews are maintained or improved upon.	▷ **4**
A 'rolling' cost based review covering all areas of material spending. Particular attention to be paid to the costs of administration, supervision and supplies. Management should be prepared to tackle 'soft' areas (eg education) as well as 'hard' areas (eg transport).	▷ **6**
Selecting for review only those areas with 'payback' potential. Areas of greatest materiality, or those which have known problems or with a history of significant improvement in other organisations should be considered first. 'Pilot' studies are useful to ensure that limited review resources are not wasted. Studies should cross departmental boundaries, for areas such as transport, to ascertain scope for pooling.	▷ **6**

Part I Background and Concepts

1 Why Value for Money is important now

'Annual income twenty pounds, annual expenditure nine-teen, nineteen six, result happiness. Annual income twenty pounds, annual expenditure twenty pounds ought and six, result misery.'
Mr Micawber   David Copperfield by Charles Dickens

CURRENT INFLUENCES IN VALUE FOR MONEY

The Economic and Social Climate

Governments in the developed world are facing serious challenges which have made politicians, management and the public more conscious of the need for achieving value for money. The demand for many of the services and programmes provided by the public sector is increasing steadily due to economic and social trends over which organisations have little control. At the same time the resources to meet these needs are limited because of the economic climate. The economic scene has been characterised by the recession, falling tax revenues from the private sector, the high cost of borrowing money, increases in the cost of raw materials and an increase in the need for the state to provide help to organisations and individuals in trouble due to the recession.

To make matters worse, support from government in the UK is being reduced in real terms; and the public is opposing steep increases in rates and taxes with the active encouragement of the media. Many organisations therefore face a bleak future, with increasingly disgruntled 'clients' and demoralised employees, unless the situation is managed economically, efficiently and effectively.

The Trend towards Greater Accountability and Disclosure

As if the hostile economic climate did not bring pressures enough, public sector organisations, and especially the local government sector in the UK, are now required to be much more accountable for their actions than before. The change in economic and political conditions over the past decade has brought a transition from an expansionary period to an age of accountability. Programmes and services are currently being put on the defensive during an era that includes government legislation to increase the powers of auditors in carrying out value for money reviews, taxpayers' revolts such as that seen in the State of California through Proposition 13, other pressure groups demanding that public officials be more openly responsible for their decisions, legislation such as the UK Local Government Planning and Land Act 1980 (which called for greater disclosure in local authority reports including the use of performance indicators) and growing scepticism about the effectiveness of certain social programmes. Cutbacks in government expenditure have become an increasingly popular political platform.

The Influence of Audit Law

The introduction of legislation to provide state and also private firms of auditors with wide powers to review the arrangements of public bodies for achieving value for money has been a particularly important development in the accountability process.

In the UK the National Audit Act 1983 provides for the Comptroller and Auditor General to review economy, efficiency and effectiveness in central government departments and other public bodies. The Local Government Finance Act 1982 states that the auditor of a municipality should satisfy himself

> that the body whose accounts are being audited has made proper arrangements for securing economy, efficiency and effectiveness in the use of resources.

It will be noted that the emphasis is on ensuring that the authority itself has made proper arrangements for achieving value for money. In other words the onus is on management not the auditor to establish the proper systems and the right climate for value for money. The Act also makes it clear that while the auditor should review the arrangements for achieving effectiveness (ie the authority's success in meeting policy objectives) he must on no account question the policies which have been decided by the democratically elected members.

This approach is followed in audit legislation in other countries, notably Sweden, Australia and Canada, where auditors may review systems for achieving effectiveness but may not criticise policy decisions. The situation is different in the USA where the General Accounting Office (GAO) has powers to review and evaluate government programmes and to suggest alternative policies where appropriate. Indeed while until recently the emphasis in the UK in value for money auditing has been on economy and efficiency, the public sector audit work in the USA has been directed principally at effectiveness, or programme evaluation as it is known. Virtually every federal department now conducts programme evaluation. Hundreds of millions of dollars are spent on evaluation activities involving thousands of agency staff years. For example, community mental health centres are required by law to set aside two percent of their annual operating budget for 'continuing evaluation of the effectiveness of programmes .... and .... for a review of the quality of the services provided by the Centre'. We discuss the subject of programme evaluation later in the book.

For the moment, it is enough to comment that it may only be a matter of time before such evaluations are carried out in public sector organisations in the UK. A situation which will lead to even more searching questions being directed at those who direct public affairs.

Adjusting to an Era of Limits

From this scenario it is clear that the challenge for the policy maker in the public sector in the 1980's is 'Managing better with less'. However, as we have indicated, many politicians and their administrators have been trained in an era of growth and are not at all sure how to go about adjusting to an era of limits. The bigger problem in the 1960's and early 1970's was how to allocate extra resources, not how to save money. The transition is perhaps made more painful by the fact that some of the civil servants and local government officers from the earlier era have been steeped in a somewhat bureaucratic and risk averse tradition whereas today's situation demands highly trained innovative management.

The task is made more daunting still due to the sheer size and complexity of most public sector authorities and as a result of legislation from central government and its effect upon the rating system. Collectively the share of government generally in total employment in OECD member countries has risen dramatically over the past twenty years, particularly in the UK where the percentage of public sector employees to the total employed has risen from 14.9% in 1960 to 21.7% in 1980. Many of the component parts of the public sector are extremely big businesses. For example, the Department of Health and Social Security employs about 90,000 people. The City of Birmingham District Council employs about 43,000 staff which is roughly the size of a large conglomerate such as the Beecham Group of Companies. Managing change on the scale that is required is therefore a very difficult task, made more so by the fact that public sector organisations are often fragmented in their structure with powerful service committees making centralised co-ordination and leadership of value for money initiatives difficult.

Compounding these problems is the difficulty many politicians and councillors have in holding their administrators accountable for delivering programmes and for following policies. The increased number of local services and programmes and the resulting growth of the bureaucracies to deliver these programmes have made it difficult for the policy makers to maintain the close personal contact they once had with the administrators. The increasingly complex and sophisticated technology used at municipal level has contributed to the problem. This situation is not helped by the poor quality of management information available to the policy makers in many organisations. This state of affairs is a legacy of the days of growth when regulating how much could be spent on individual areas was all that was demanded. In today's social and economic climate it is necessary for politicians (and administrators) to have timely and accurate performance measurement of output to ensure that programmes are not only economic and efficient but effective as well.

Public sector organisations in the UK have a well deserved international reputation for probity, dedication and regularity in conducting their affairs. They have individuals, both politicians and administrators, who have the leadership qualities, flair and determination necessary to achieve the difficult adjustment to the new era of limits. These qualities however are not sufficient in themselves. Politicians and administrators need guidance in the management techniques, systems and organisational changes required to ensure that they make the transition effectively and achieve better value for money for their organisations. We believe that this book provides this guidance in a practical way, based on the wide experience gained by Price Waterhouse over a long period in helping to achieve value for money at all levels of government in most developing countries in the world. In particular, the book sets out to show that in even the best run organisations, idle resources can be identified and made available to meet more deserving needs and services.

The book will help public bodies to set up a framework for action and help them to evaluate such questions as whether:

1) There are more economical ways of meeting required service levels.
2) The organisation is being managed well.
3) The organisation is getting what it is paying for.
4) All of the present services are necessary.
5) New services and activities need to be developed.
6) The performance measurement and budgeting systems are providing the policy makers with adequate and timely information to help them achieve value for money.

These are all questions which governments, auditors, citizens and special interest groups are increasingly asking of the public sector − questions to which there are often no immediate answers at present.

We appreciate that there is no single 'right way' to run an organisation, particularly one as complex as a government department or local authority. The policies and priorities of each must differ according to the nature of its programmes, the environment in which it works and its own ethos and culture. Nevertheless, there are certain basic ground rules for achieving value for money which apply in any organisation and it is these we have attempted to identify and explain. For the value for money professional we hope that the book will add considerably to the debate in what is a rapidly evolving field. For the busy politician and administrator the 'action plan' at the front of the book will direct him or her to the particular areas they may be interested in if they do not wish to read the material in full. Also Chapter 12 contains a series of key point questionnaires for use by politicians and senior officers to quickly get a 'feel' as to whether areas crucial to good value for money, such as manpower management, are being handled effectively.

2   What is Value for Money?

'Do not buy what you want but what you need, what you do not need is dear at a farthing'.

Cato

Value for money is of concern to all those involved in the public sector; that is the politicians and administrators who manage its various organisations, and the public who both contribute to and benefit from the services they provide. It is achieved by planning, reporting upon and reviewing performance on the basis of clear, unambiguous statements of policy objectives or goals. Value for money is therefore an expression of the economy, the efficiency and the effectiveness with which all institutions, large and small, operate in the public sector.

Parliament, ministers, permanent secretaries, electors, councillors, ratepayers and all levels of management at both central and local level should be accountable for their actions. Public accountability is an important part of the functioning of our democratic political system. Public sector accountability means that those charged with drafting and/or carrying out policy should be obliged to give an explanation of their activities to their electorate.

An important element of public sector accountability is the need for:

> . . . adopting managerial practices that will promote the efficiency and effectiveness of non-commercial entities; by the establishment of an appropriate budgetary framework.
> (D. Neald 'Public Expenditure')

The definition recognises that the majority of public expenditure is not primarily financed by charges to users but rather by budgetary appropriations. It is this notion of accountability that has led to the more colloquial expression: VALUE FOR MONEY. As Sir Edward du Cann, a former chairman of the Public Accounts Committee, told the House of Commons:

> . . .the control of public expenditure is near the top of the charts recording the public interests.

This interest is not peculiar to the UK, it is now pursued in every advanced western country. Australia and Canada have both had Royal Commissions reporting upon the reform of their financial management and both, along with several other countries, have legislated to provide expanded public sector audit mandates.

Definitions

Being a colloquialism, value for money has become a wide and ambiguous term, but it is generally accepted that it covers three basic elements: economy, efficiency and effectiveness. All three terms are now commonplace in the literature. They are defined as follows:

Economy   The practice by management of the virtues of thrift and good housekeeping. An economical operation acquires resources in appropriate quality and quantity at the lowest cost.

A lack of economy could occur, for example, when there is overstaffing or when overpriced facilities are used.

Efficiency   Making sure that the maximum useful output is gained from the resources devoted to each activity, or, alternatively, that only the minimum level of resources are devoted to achieving a given level of output.

An operation could be said to have increased in efficiency if either lower costs were used to produce a given amount of output, or a given level of cost resulted in increased output. Inefficiency would be revealed by identifying the performance of work with no useful purpose, or the accumulation of an excess of material and supplies.

Effectiveness   Ensuring that the output from any given activity (or the impact that services have on a community) is achieving the desired results.

To evaluate effectiveness we need to establish that approved/desired goals are being achieved. A goal (or operating objective) may be defined as a concrete expression of a policy objective. This is not necessarily a straightforward procedure; some goals may not be initially apparent. Once a set of goals has been established we need to determine whether these goals are being accomplished. By way of example the overall policy objective for a Parks and Recreation department might be to 'provide adequate leisure facilities and open space'. One of the goals or operating objectives could be 'maintain buildings, playing fields, trees and roadsides'.

The three elements, economy, efficiency and effectiveness, have been ranked in order of scope and ease of measurement although they are clearly interrelated to one another. This view is shared by the Chartered Institute of Public Finance and Accountancy (CIPFA) in the UK who emphasise that the attainment of economy and efficiency is of little practical use if effectiveness is disregarded. CIPFA's Standards for the External Audit of Local Authorities state:

> Economy and efficiency in the execution of programmes is of small consequence if the programmes are not meeting the authority's objectives and no assessment of value for money is complete without regard to effectiveness. In order to assess effectiveness, it is necessary first to determine and specify the objectives and second, to assess performance against these objectives so that appropriate adjustment or remedial action can be taken.

Economy

To establish economy of operation means that management should establish internal regulations for the creation of standards, establishment levels etc. For example there should be a strict review procedure covering the need to re-fill any post which becomes vacant.

There are two aspects to establishing economical services: quality and cost. Quality of materials may be set out in technical specifications or professional guidelines. Quality, or perhaps calibre, of staff may also be provided by professional guidelines or perhaps an employment agreement. Once quality of resources has been established, management need to ensure that they are obtained at minimum or 'acceptable' cost, in relation to local conditions of operation. This last point may be important. For example, if there is a shortage of a particular specialist or grade of staff it may only be possible to employ someone who is over, rather than under, skilled.

Efficiency

Efficiency is harder to verify. The definition implies that we can measure output per unit of input (eg cost per planning application processed), but this may not be so easily quantified in practice. However, in recognition of the need for a meaningful national comparison of efficiency, in terms of units processed, various research studies have been undertaken. In the UK, for example, the Chartered Institute of Public Finance and Accountancy have developed a range of comparative statistics for all major local authority services. This statistical service has been used by the Audit Commission for Local Government in England and Wales to provide comparative data for the so-called 'cluster' analysis ie an analysis by authorities grouped together in categories determined by certain demographic and economic criteria. This analysis is discussed in more detail in chapter 6.

The 1981 Canadian Audit Guide discussed the importance of efficiency measurements in the following terms:

> Standards and performance data are used for different purposes in various information and control systems. These are to:
> - demonstrate achievement of results by comparing performance data to standards, targets and goals;
> - plan operations and budget resource requirements by providing data for comparing present and proposed methods and procedures;
> - provide a rational basis for pricing goods and services (when charges are made);
> - to make trade-off decisions between efficiency and the level of service; and

  − indicate to employees and supervisors what results are
  expected.

It will be seen then that standards are useful both in appraising the
performance of managers and groups of employees and in
motivating them.

The key elements that therefore arise from management
adopting efficiency measures are:

1) *An awareness of desired goals* − and the determination to
  accomplish them in the most economical and efficient manner;
2) *A need to plan operations* − as efficiently as possible for a
  given level of resources (or budgeted level of income if a
  statutory authority is expected to largely generate its own
  income);
3) *The need for a structured organisation* − whose administration
  should follow prescribed work measures and procedures in
  order to avoid duplication of effort, unnecessary tasks, idle
  time; and
4) *The provision of work instructions* − in sufficient detail, to
  employees who are suitably qualified and trained for the duties
  they are required to perform.

The measurement of efficiency should not be thought of as an end
in itself. Improving efficiency is the objective. By developing
efficiency measures management can contribute to improving it
and to specifying the expected gains from suggested improvements. Management should be encouraged to monitor efficiency
on a regular basis rather than as an ad hoc exercise.

Effectiveness

Irrespective of the resources used in an activity, management
should primarily be concerned with the results obtained − how
effective is the activity? It could be that effectiveness might be
obtained more efficiently and, conversely, it could be that, despite the hard working efforts of those involved, a particular
activity is ineffective. For example, members of a mobile clinic
could be very efficient in administering a school's inoculation

programme but its effectiveness could be called into question if there was no perceptible decrease in the illness being inoculated against. Well intentioned effort and resources would have been wasted.

As we implied earlier, managers, whilst being concerned for the manner in which a programme is implemented, should primarily be concerned with the results achieved. In some instances it may be possible to produce quantitative data to monitor progress; in other instances it may be that the perceived value of a service will have to be measured by indirect means, for example, via a user survey.

The effectiveness indicators developed by management cannot be the same therefore as those developed to measure efficiency. For example, a government grant programme, designed to encourage the re-deployment of industry to economically depressed areas, should not be assessed in terms of effectiveness by the number of firms that re-locate or by the total amount of grants paid. These are efficiency measures only. One could only determine, from such measures, the success (in work-load terms) of management in attracting firms to move location. To measure and monitor effectiveness, management would have to use other measures, such as the reduction in the number of unemployed in the assisted areas.

In the many instances when effectiveness can only be indicated by personal opinions or judgement, it is important to be seen to be taking reasonable steps to avoid bias. Management should endeavour to obtain their information from third-parties such as independent specialists or by means of consumer surveys.

Thunder Bay

A useful approach to monitoring Value for Money has been developed by the City of Thunder Bay, Ontario, Canada. The city is committed to the advancement of modern management systems and performance measures. In 1980 the City's Chief Administrative Officer received the International City Management's Innovation Award for Organisation and Management. The City's Corporate Planning and Development Division have categorised performance measures into three groups:

Workload/Demand Measures: to indicate the amount of work
  done or to be done;
Economy/Efficiency Measures: to measure how well resources
  are utilised; and
Effectiveness Measures: to measure how well a goal or objective
  is being achieved.

Under this system each department is divided into programme
areas and a detailed programme description is provided. Performance measures are provided under each category together with
details of the source of information, how it is to be collected, how
it is to be analysed (manual/computer), and the frequency of data
collection (which ranges from annually to daily). Each programme, and its funding, is discussed with the responsible manager and agreed by him.

This approach was originally linked to a programme based
budgeting system, however, since 1979 the city has adopted Zero
Based budgeting. Both of these advanced budgeting techniques,
which entail a critical questioning of activities under each budget
head, are discussed in Chapter 8.

Figure 2.1 reproduces two of Thunder Bay's programmes.
Note that, just as it can be difficult to measure effectiveness by
other than objective means, it may well be impossible to measure
efficiency − as in the second case illustrated, which deals with
police community relations.

Efficiency and Effectiveness − need they conflict?

A conflict can arise between efficiency and effectiveness. For
example, the ratepayer is on the one hand concerned with the
effectiveness of the services he receives from his local authority.
On the other hand he is concerned about the level of contribution
he has to make. As Noel Hepworth, Director of the Chartered
Institute of Public Finance and Accountancy, states:

> The conflict between efficiency and effectiveness, par-
> ticularly in sensitive services like education and social ser-
> vices, is extremely difficult to resolve, and is best left to
> individual judgements, which really means the judgement of
> those most concerned with the development of the service.

The City of Thunder Bay
1980 PERFORMANCE MEASUREMENT PROJECT

DATE ___December 31, 1980___

PAGE ___1___

DEPARTMENT	PROGRAM AREA	SIGNATURE
LIBRARY	BOOKMOBILE	Grover Burgis, Chief Librarian

PROGRAM DESCRIPTION

To operate a bookmobile vehicle to provide book-borrowing services at sites away from the central Resource Libraries.

COLLECTION FREQUENCY CODE

1 Annual	4 Monthly
2 Bi-annual	5 Weekly
3 Quarterly	6 Daily

	PERFORMANCE MEASUREMENTS	SOURCE AND HOW COLLECTED	HOW ANALYSED OPTIONS	COLL. FREQ CODE
WORKLOAD/ DEMAND	– number of miles per year – number of stops per week – number of stop hours per week – number of patrons served per year – number of books borrowed per year – number of new library members enrolled, per year	internal records " " " " " " " " " "	Manual " " " " "	4 4 4 4 4 4
EFFICIENCY	– gross operating cost per mile – gross operating cost per stop hour – gross Cost per circulated volume	approved Budgets, internal records " " " " " "	Manual " "	1 1 1
EFFECTIVENESS	– percentage of users that rate service as satisfactory	User survey	Manual	1

111

T8205IA

FIGURE 2.1

The City of Thunder Bay

1980 PERFORMANCE MEASUREMENT PROJECT

DATE December 31, 1980
PAGE 5

DEPARTMENT POLICE

PROGRAM AREA COMMUNITY RELATIONS

SIGNATURE Tom Keep – Chief of Police

PROGRAM DESCRIPTION
Co-ordination of safety programs in schools.
Co-ordination of community relations programs.
Crime prevention programs.

COLLECTION FREQUENCY CODE

1 Annual	4 Monthly
2 Bi-annual	5 Weekly
3 Quarterly	6 Daily

	PERFORMANCE MEASUREMENTS	SOURCE AND HOW COLLECTED	HOW ANALYSED OPTIONS	COLL. FREQ CODE
WORKLOAD/ DEMAND	– police public relation contact – Crime Prevention and Safety programs in schools – Community police media communications	internal records internal records internal records	Man-Comp Man-Comp Man-Comp	4 4 & 1 4
EFFICIENCY				
EFFECTIVENESS	– % of requests for safety presentations satisfied – % of satisfactorily resolved complaints – degree of community support – Media communications per week – % of citizens feeling safe walking in the neighbourhoods at night – Preprogram incidence of crime X in area Y minus post program – Incidence of crime X in area Y – Preprogram incidence of crime X in area Y	internal records internal records internal records survey internal records internal records	Manual Manual Manual Computer Manual Manual	4 4 4 1 4 4

TB2051A

110

FIGURE 2.1 continued

Hepworth's view can best be illustrated by two examples. Consider first a non-sensitive area — a Parks Department; management would wish to see that gardeners and groundsmen did their best with the funds available to provide recreational facilities for the general public. The effectiveness of the various programmes undertaken would be subjective — it would be a matter of general public opinion whether or not the facilities provided were well maintained and provided pleasure. Efficiency might perhaps be improved; this could: (i) lead to cost savings which probably would have little impact on effectiveness or (ii) lead to cost redeployment which might improve consumer satisfaction. In any event management's main consideration is to do as good a job as possible for a given level of funding.

Secondly, consider a sensitive area — a hospital's Accident and Emergency Department, where the prime requirement is for an effective service. An ineffective service may lead to unnecessary loss of life. One of the contentious issues that presently arise in certain parts of the National Health Service is that if fewer resources are available there is a considerable pressure to improve efficiency and to some extent to carry a higher risk over the effectiveness of a service. Efficiency is clearly important but for some programmes effectiveness is the paramount consideration. Casualty staff may have long periods of inactivity but this is the consequence of providing an effective service, as demanded by the public.

These two examples tend to hide a conflict that has generally been ignored by management, ie that all those involved in either the provision or receipt of services from public sector institutions do not necessarily have similar expectations. Politicians, with re-election always in mind, tend to look to a short term horizon (the next election) by which time they wish to achieve results. Management are more concerned with longer term success. Members of the public are in the anomolous position of, on the one hand, demanding better provision and higher quality of services whilst, on the other, not wishing to make additional contributions. Social values and attitudes equally influence the public. Public opinion on what might be termed 'topical' programmes, such as the general quality of health care, the price of electricity, the level of defence expenditure, and so on receive wide publicity. By contrast, less attention is given to lesser funded 'acute' programmes such as for the mentally ill, drug addiction or the provision of overseas aid.

The potential for efficiency and effectiveness to be in conflict therefore depends upon two factors:

1) Whether the programme is in a sensitive area;
2) The expectations of all those involved in either the provision or receipt of the service.

Having indicated the possibility of conflict it should be stated that it is also possible to have programmes that, besides being the most economical and efficient, are very effective. For example, consider the provision of accommodation for children in care. For many children there are usually two alternatives − they may either reside in residential homes or they may be boarded out with foster parents. The latter alternative is by far the cheaper and is also increasingly being regarded as the more beneficial to the children.

A further example illustrates the distinction. Consider a project to construct a new by-pass. Efficiency in carrying out the task of building the road would be represented by a cost per mile, completion to timetable or similar measure. But effectiveness would be represented by the extent to which the by-pass achieved its planned objectives of reducing travel time, accidents, disturbance to the local community and transport costs. In this illustration one is dealing with different levels of management. In measuring efficiency (cost per mile) it is really the performance of the project engineer that is being evaluated. He is not responsible for the project achieving its objectives. In measuring effectiveness one is evaluating the decisions of those responsible for choosing the project, ie has the by-pass reduced travel costs etc, or is it a highly economical and efficient white elephant?

Barriers to Value for Money

Many barriers must be overcome in order to achieve VFM. These include: politics, weak governing bodies, tradition, lack of motivation, and lack of education and training programmes.

There is a conflict that all politicians face; that is, the trade-off between constituency interests and national priorities. These may often not be the same and as, presumably, the politician wishes future re-election his opinions may, not unnaturally, be biased. Churchill may well have said 'Democracy is the worst form of government' but he did add ' — except all others.' Politicians are inevitable and necessary in a democracy but individual and party political influences need to be monitored by committees and working parties whose deliberations help provide a more impartial contribution to parliamentary debate.

Successive British governments have failed to legislate for administrative reform. The present (Conservative) UK Government has only indirectly introduced measures that may lead to administrative and budgetary reform. In summary their actions have included:

1) Since 1981, a change in the basis of planning public expenditure from 'volume' to cash.
2) The introduction of cash limits and, for local authorities, rate capping, ie setting levels for increases in rates.
3) The introduction of statutory VFM audit requirements for much of the public sector. Nationalised industries are a notable exception.

Particularly since the introduction of cash limits, there is an implied assumption that keeping within a cash target denotes a well run department. This is not necessarily true, cash accounting only deals with fiscal compliance, it says nothing about whether VFM is being achieved.

The traditional approach to selecting management in the public sector is that technically qualified people are often designated as departmental heads. To continue with the Health Service analogy, often a medical specialist is in charge of a particular department because he is technically very competent. However, he may not be able to co-ordinate the activities of his fellow clinicians and support staff in attaining the best use of resources available to them. Traditionally the primary qualification for a departmental manager is that he be a good administrator. To improve this situation, technical specialists should receive training in basic management techniques as a pre-requisite for certain career paths. Motivation, to achieve value for money, must come from the top. It can prove a fruitless task developing systems to achieve levels of performance not demanded. All too often, what has been called 'entrenched lethargy' or empire building provide obstacles to the achievement of VFM. Considerable courage, expertise and determination are required by top management therefore to break down these barriers. The remainder of this book hopefully will provide management with some pointers on how to do this.

3 Elements of Good Practice

'Unless you have people within an organisation who wish to bring about changes. . .then you will not achieve|the changes; unless the spark is from within you will not have change.'

Sir Derek Rayner

This chapter considers the main elements of good VFM practice and the principal steps any public sector organisation needs to take to establish the right framework for action. We shall only touch on each of these elements at this stage because we describe them in greater detail in succeeding chapters. This chapter therefore may be considered as a 'map' which will help management at all levels to chart their course in organising value for money arrangements. Not that what we have to say is meant to be the last word on how to achieve value for money since it is very much an evolving subject. It will however add to the debate and hopefully lay down the ground rules for public organisations whether large or small.

It cannot be stressed enough that value for money is not just a collection of techniques. It is above all an attitude of mind, a commitment to good practice on the part of politicians and officials. It is particularly important for management to instil a positive approach towards achieving value for money at all levels, so that the commitment permeates the whole organisation. Having said that, value for money cannot be achieved by merely inspiring the organisation with the necessary crusading spirit. Management's enthusiasm and drive has to be supported by the right organisational structure and also formalised budgeting, evaluation and monitoring systems. Naturally, enthusiasm at all levels will be encouraged if there is a system for financially rewarding anyone who provides a worthwhile suggestion for improving value for money.

What constitutes the 'right' system and structure must vary depending upon the nature of the organisation and its size.

FIGURE 3.1 *14 Key point action plan for securing Value for Money*

1 Total commitment by senior elected representatives and officials. Right attitude to achieving VFM should permeate whole organisation.
2 Small, powerful but representative committee to direct and co-ordinate Value for Money projects. Corporate approach to VFM should be adopted.
3 Clearly defined strategic and operational objectives and targets for all functions and activities.
4 Priority based or zero based budgeting approach whereby budget items are ranked for priority and the incremental effects of service level changes are calculated.
5 Key performance measures used for all major functions to evaluate and monitor productivity and effectiveness.
6 Performance measures linked to performance targets or standards for operational management so that productivity gains achieved during VFM reviews are maintained or improved upon.
7 A 'rolling' cost based review covering all areas of material spending and linked to the budgeting process. Particular attention to be paid to the costs of administration and supervision, energy and supplies. Management should be prepared to tackle 'soft' areas (eg education) as well as 'hard' areas (eg transport).
8 Regular comparisons with the costs and performance applying in the private sector for all services where it is appropriate to do so. Where better cost effectiveness can be obtained outside the organisation managers should be asked to justify keeping the service in-house.
9 Select for review only those areas with 'payback' potential. Areas of greatest materiality, or those which have known problems or those with a history of significant improvement in other organisations, should be considered first. 'Pilot' studies are useful to ensure that limited review resources are not wasted. Studies should cross departmental boundaries, for areas such as transport, to ascertain what scope exists for 'pooling'.
10 Investment made in people or equipment which will save money within a reasonable payback period (ideally 2/3 years) eg energy conservation officers and monitoring equipment, contract audit specialists, 'cook-chill' catering equipment.
11 Effective procedures to ensure that there is a proper control over scarce resources, eg for identifying surplus land, overstocking, unbanked cash, overmanning.
12 Consumer and 'client' surveys on a sample basis to test the quality of services eg 'exit' questionnaires for mature students.
13 Budget process to encourage the controlled use of virement. Other incentives to achieving VFM such as performance bonuses should be considered.
14 Officials should be trained in management as well as technical matters.

Nevertheless certain key elements have to be in place whether the organisation operates at central, regional or local level. Figure 3.1 shows a 14 key point Action Plan for securing value for money for politicians, senior officers and other decision takers at European, national, regional and local level.

The key points in the action plan are discussed in turn later in the chapter. First however, we group them into their main elements as follows:

Define clearly the strategy and objectives   Specify them for each service or programme and communicate these clearly to management. If this task is not done adequately there is nothing against which to measure either Value for Money or particularly the effectiveness with which policy objectives are delivered.

Introduce a comprehensive budgeting process   A discipline which not only controls spending but which challenges the underlying assumptions in the main spending areas. In particular the budgetary process should provide management with the means of judging the effect of reducing, eliminating or increasing service levels in both quantitative and qualitative terms. The system should also provide the means of ranking, in a reasonably scientific way, the conflicting priorities of various service activities.

Establish a continuous 'rolling' cost based review process   Such a review would imply a critical questioning of all major spending areas and concentrate particularly on key resource costs such as energy, supplies and above all manning which should be reviewed in the light of changing activity levels and for opportunities to purchase the services more cheaply in the private sector ('contracting out').

Provide an effective monitoring process   Checking to ensure that the economy, efficiency and effectiveness of each main function or programme is maintained or improved following the cost based review process. An important feature of the monitoring system

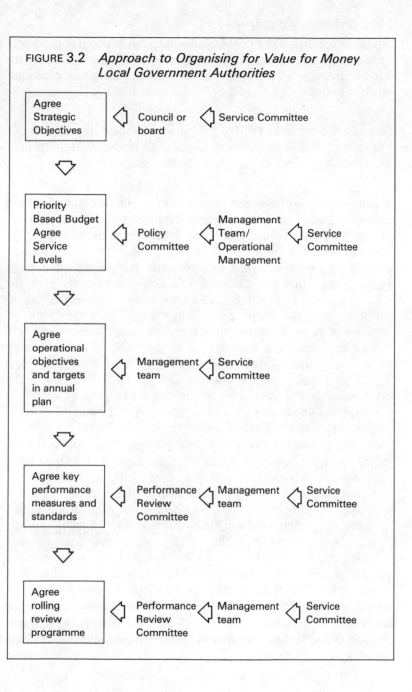

FIGURE 3.2 *Approach to Organising for Value for Money Local Government Authorities*

Agree Strategic Objectives ◁ Council or board ◁ Service Committee

▽

Priority Based Budget Agree Service Levels ◁ Policy Committee ◁ Management Team/ Operational Management ◁ Service Committee

▽

Agree operational objectives and targets in annual plan ◁ Management team ◁ Service Committee

▽

Agree key performance measures and standards ◁ Performance Review Committee ◁ Management team ◁ Service Committee

▽

Agree rolling review programme ◁ Performance Review Committee ◁ Management team ◁ Service Committee would be the use of key performance measures linked to predetermined operating targets or standards to ensure that management had an effective control over productivity in the light of changing work volumes.

Ensure effective use of the organisation's resources   This involves establishing procedures to achieve the best utilisation of land and property, manpower, stores, current assets.

Develop a strong management structure   One which provides powerful leadership at the top to ensure that VFM improvements are followed through. A suitable mechanism, for example, is often a small but powerful Performance Review Committee of elected members working closely with the management team (through the Chief Executive) in liaison with the service committees, supported by specialist VFM resources. The way in which VFM might be organised is shown in Figure 3.2

None of these elements are in themselves sufficient to provide the right framework with which to achieve value for money because they each draw strength from the others. For example, a zero based budgeting process would be ineffective without a continuous cost based review process to help question basic assumptions about cost. It will be seen too that value for money implies much more than a crude cost cutting exercise. As we have said earlier, it has as much to do with judging the quality and level of service and assessing whether programme objectives have been satisfactorily delivered, as with pure cost considerations.

A vigorous VFM programme can nevertheless uncover significant savings in even the best run organisations. An example of this is the review carried out at Dudley Metropolitan Borough, in the West Midlands, possibly the most comprehensive cost based review yet carried out in a local authority. At Dudley a systematic review of each service run by the Council lead to annual savings equivalent to 7% of the annual revenue 'spend' of around £80m. These savings were made in a Borough which by all accepted indicators (eg number of council staff per 1,000 population), was already one of the most economical and efficient authorities in the country.

Manpower Costs

In considering these elements and particularly cost based reviews, it must be stressed at the outset that in most public sector undertakings, manpower costs account for between 60% and 70% of total expenditure. Inevitably therefore significant savings from value for money initiatives will lead to social consequences including the redeployment, early retirement and even redundancy of staff. Consequently it is important that management are prepared to deal with possible staff cuts before they set out to undertake VFM programmes. Even though experience shows that large savings can be achieved without forced redundancy, through careful phasing of staff reductions and a sympathetic approach, a certain amount of upheaval is inevitable.

Many governmental authorities both in the UK and in Europe operate a strict 'no-redundancy' policy even in areas where a major falling off in activity (eg capital spending) would justify a similar reduction in manning. This raises the question as to whether the cost of operating such 'no-redundancy' policies should be clearly identified and notified to the taxpayer on whom the burden falls. It is difficult to see, regardless of political viewpoint, how the carrying of unnecessary overheads can be justified when the saving from their elimination could be used either to reduce taxes or alternatively to increase the resources available to other hard pressed services. These matters are discussed in more detail in Chapter 5.

It is noticeable that the majority of VFM reviews carried out in the public sector so far have been directed at fairly non-contentious areas such as purchasing and stores, transport and energy costs. Furthermore, where manpower costs have been tackled, they have been in what Professor Tomkins of Bath University calls the 'hard areas where relatively unambiguous goals and performance measures can be set' eg refuse collection, upkeep of parks, building maintenance etc. However, it is in the 'soft' areas such as social services and education where it becomes difficult to measure manpower needs and where indeed the largest expenditure often lies. These 'soft' areas have to be brought within the orbit of the review process if significant improvements are to be made. At Dudley for example the bulk of the savings came from 'non-operational' manning areas in the Social Services, Education and Housing departments. This review and similar studies such as that carried out for the Social Services department at the City of Birmingham, have proved that significant savings can be found in these high spend 'soft areas'. The Birmingham review alone identified savings of over £1 million per year without any adverse effect upon service levels.

Setting Objectives

The entire framework for achieving VFM rests upon the organisation setting clear policy objectives for each activity or programme. Without clear objectives and aims it becomes impossible to measure the effectiveness of the organisation in achieving its goals. In practice these objectives would be expressed at several different levels:

Overall aims of the organisation   A very broad view of where the organisation is headed. A broad aim might be 'To provide for the development of industry, warehousing and service users in order to satisfy the employment needs of the local population', or 'To formulate a strategy to deal with the rising number of the over 75's'.

Medium to short term operational objectives   These would be incorporated in a strategic plan covering a number of years. There would also be an annual plan which would summarise for the organisation as a whole and for each committee and service:

- resources to be allocated for the year, capital, revenue and people
- results expected in terms of service outputs and results
- service levels
- specific objectives to be achieved. Objectives expressed at this level could be for example, to implement the rent arrears control strategy' or, 'to review the effectiveness and efficiency of Social Services Transport'.

Operational targets   At this level objectives would be expressed as quantitative targets to be achieved by operational management and linked to performance measures and standards. For example, to achieve 96% occupancy of long stay places in residential homes, to reduce the level of rent arrears for previous tenants by 2½%, or to reduce energy costs in specific buildings by 10% in 1984/85.

Such a hierarchy of objectives and targets would be set for the council or public sector service as a whole. It would form the basis for subsequent evaluation and monitoring of the VFM arrangements, and, more specifically, determining whether the laid down goals had been met effectively. As we have already implied the VFM process is a circular one and the existing service objectives and targets would be modified and refined partly as a result of other VFM elements, particularly the continuous review process and the use of performance measures. An example of 'good practice' in the setting of different levels of objectives and targets at a local government level is that of the London Borough of Bexley which is illustrated in the Appendix to this chapter.

The Budget Process

Financial control systems are, to a very large extent, a function of their social and organisational environment. Until recently therefore officials have thought it somewhat pointless to develop systems aimed at achieving levels of performance which are not demanded. Officials have been happy to go along with accountability, legality and probity whilst keeping within the budgets allotted to them. However, they are now faced with becoming more accountable for operational and financial management especially during the budgeting process.

Public sector budgets in the past have invariably been developed on a largely incremental basis, ie adding a percentage for inflation to last year's budget which otherwise remains the same apart from the need to respond to legislative influences. Latterly however, pressures on spending, for example in the form of 'cash limits', have forced management not only to make more scientifically based ranking decisions on the use of resources but have caused them to question much more critically the underlying assumptions upon which the budget is based, particularly in terms of traditional service levels and programme outputs.

These developments have caused management to seek improvements in two particular areas:

1) The management structure
2) The quality of management information; and especially the budgetary control system.

All too often in the public sector, organisational structures are not kept in line with functional responsibilities. Before an effective management information system can be introduced therefore it is necessary to ensure that budget statements for individual managers contain only cost information for activities over which the manager has effective control and, furthermore, that the manager is reasonably close to the activities. The more remote the budget holders from their activities and clients, the less likely they are to be able to secure improvements in value for money.

Aside from these organisational considerations, however, the budget process in the public sector is becoming increasingly sophisticated to take account of a detailed questioning of both the cost and efficiency of each activity (the cost based review process) and more fundamentally the critical analysis of whether activities, programmes or services are justified, and, if so, whether they should be continued at lower (or perhaps higher) levels. These questions can be raised in a structured way through such techniques as Programme, Planning and Budgeting Systems or Zero Based Budgeting which seek to provide (1) a method of showing the incremental effect of different levels of service options, and (2) a scientific method of prioritising apparently conflicting claims for resources.

While there has been widespread disappointment over the results of Zero Based Budgeting in the public sector there appears to be a growing acceptance that a scaled down, less bureaucratic version, which nonetheless imposes the discipline of questioning basic assumptions and custom and practice, can be made worthwhile. This type of alternative budgeting strategy is discussed in more detail in Chapter 8. In that chapter we also discuss recent technological developments such as the use of microcomputers and the application of modelling packages to assist budget makers in asking crucial 'what if' questions.

Cost Based Reviews

An important component of VFM arrangements is the setting up of a strategic programme covering say 4 or 5 years for the cost based review on a continuous cycle of each main budget heading. This cycle should be linked with the budget process and particularly the systematic review of service levels. In selecting and prioritising areas for review it is necessary to concentrate on areas of materiality and/or of known concern using the organisation's budget as the starting point. Other sources of topics for review will include:

1) Those highlighted by reference to performance measures using comparisons with other organisations of similar economic, demographic and geographic background, and with the private sector.
2) Areas identified through scope reviews by internal and external auditors and other bodies.
3) Knowledge of savings made in similar organisations eg privatisation of refuse collection, cost rationalisation of non-ambulance transport in the health services.
4) Areas where legislation or other changes dictate revisions to the scope of a service.
5) Areas where legislation directs a review should be carried out.

It is important that once a cost based review programme is developed, it is regarded as being flexible and is capable of being changed to meet altered circumstances. Resources for carrying out reviews are limited and it is essential that only areas which offer 'payback' are selected. In this regard the use of a 'pilot' study of a selected area is helpful to cut down the risk of time being wasted on an unfruitful project. A pilot study may take say four or five days in a typical local government department. The time would be spent interviewing senior officials, in carrying out cost and performance comparisons to confirm or otherwise that an area justifies the use of investigative resources and also to ensure that clear terms of reference are established. If no topics showing potential for improvement are found then the study team should move on to more promising areas.

Scope of Reviews

The scope of the reviews themselves should be balanced, comprehensive and cover each of the 3 E's, economy, efficiency and effectiveness. The cost based review would normally take account of:

1) The policy objectives, how their effectiveness is measured and what action is taken if policy objectives are not being met.
2) The yardsticks and efficiency measures used by the department itself to control its activities and to ensure that economy and efficiency are achieved.
3) The financial and other budgeting and control procedures used within the department or function.
4) The organisational structure and staffing levels.
5) Activity levels.
6) Overhead costs.
7) Each main procedure/activity/function within the department, with a view to asking:
    a) Is it necessary?
    b) Can it be carried out more efficiently?
    c) Can it be carried out at less cost without impairing service?
    d) Can it be carried out more cheaply elsewhere in the organisation or outside by private enterprise?
    e) Is there scope for 'pooling' ie sharing joint transport or computer facilities with other locations.

Performance Measures

A particularly useful analytical tool in the investigation of value for money is the performance measure. Performance Measures are derived by linking the input of an activity to its output to provide a product such as cost per planning application processed or cost per 1,000 population of library services. They can be designed for evaluating not only economy and efficiency (cost per planning application processed) but also the effectiveness of programmes, for example, fire service response times. Ideally they should be designed on a hierarchical basis so that costs and service outputs are tested at successively lower levels until the apparent root cause of a problem is established. While such indicators can only pose questions and not solve problems they are useful in directing attention to areas of potential improvement. They are also of considerable assistance in the budget making process and in particular in helping to assess the incremental effect of varying service levels.

Monitoring Performance

The use of Performance Measures is also an important tool in the subsequent monitoring of an activity once the review process has been completed. Indeed an important output from a cost based review is the setting of performance standards for subsequent use in the monitoring process. It should be added that Performance Measures should not be the only source of information used to assess productivity, and that so far as possible a means of cross checking should be found. In the case of an architect's department for example, a second check might be the regular comparison of notional fees earned by the department (based on private sector fee scales) with the department's costs.

In the case of say a local government authority it is suggested that a set of not more than 6 key performance measures should be developed in the annual plan for each service covering economy, efficiency and also effectiveness. For example, an efficiency measure for library assistants might be the number of book issues per hour. A measure of economy might be cost per hectare of ground maintained while an effectiveness measure might be the removal of abandoned vehicles within 48 hours of notification to the appropriate department. At a higher level an effectiveness measure for a government sponsored vocational training scheme might be '% of trainees placed successfully in training related employment'. Ideally such measures would always be related to predetermined standards (eg turnaround time on planning applications not to exceed x weeks) to provide management with targeted performance upon which the efficiency of operations could be judged and which might be used as a basis for deciding promotion prospects or salary levels.

Effectiveness measures naturally contain an element of subjectivity and the only way to collect the necessary data may be by user or consumer survey (eg to ascertain the % of leisure centre users satisfied with the scope and availability of services). The use of sample user surveys is fairly widespread in the USA and Canada, through such agencies as the Dayton Public Opinion Center, but the technique has not been used to the same extent in Europe. A further technique, trained observer ratings, provides another method of testing the effectiveness of public services such as cleansing and refuse collection. This system entails setting up predetermined visual standards against which the trained observer measures the effectiveness of the particular service.

There are some activities which are measurable and repetitive even in 'soft' areas as was shown in the use of statistics in a school in Long Island which lead to a 55% reduction in teachers' absenteeism. However, care has to be taken in using performance measures in areas where a high degree of personal judgement is involved because morale and motivation may be destroyed by an over-emphasis on efficiency measures. This does not mean that staff in social services or education will inevitably reject such measures, especially if they can be persuaded that a review of efficiency could be beneficial. For example if money saved on inessential items, say by a better pooling of transport facilities or from reduced energy costs, could be channelled into more fruitful areas such as providing a better meals-on-wheels service to the aged. This redeployment of money does of course rely on there being an effective system of virement to allow underspends on one budget head to be transferred to another.

The use of performance measures therefore is an important component of an organisation's overall management information system not only for evaluating services but also in monitoring the productivity and effectiveness of departments against predetermined targets, and/or by reference to other authorities and past trends.

One particular use of performance measures is in the comparison of performance or productivity with the private sector. A regular comparison to private sector costs should be made by senior management for all services which are capable in theory of being 'contracted out' or even privatised. Conversely, already contracted out services such as legal advice and printing services might be carried out more economically (or effectively) in-house and these services should also be kept under review.

Measuring Manpower Productivity

Further areas upon which to focus the use of performance measures during cost based reviews are administrative and supervisory staff costs. While performance measures and other productivity monitoring systems have been used extensively in the direct labour (or blue collar) area they have been relatively little used in the administrative area.

Indeed productivity gains in the administrative area have lagged far behind those in the 'production' area, and while labour forces providing the front line services have generally been sharply reduced, the administrative 'tail' has often remained intact or even increased in size. These claims are supported in figure 3.3. It is important that measurement should not be confined to the evaluation of lower level posts. Often one finds that unnecessary 'tiers' of management exist which are often the residual effect of past re-organisation or of service objectives the reason for which has long since disappeared. A more detailed discussion of the important topic of performance measurement is contained in chapter 4.

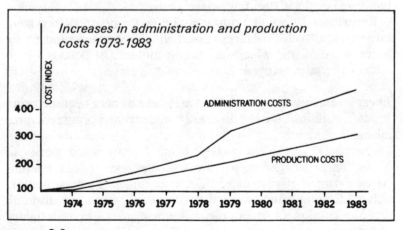

FIGURE 3.3

Control over Resources

A further area in the fight for VFM is the setting of control procedures to ensure the efficient use of resources such as energy, land and buildings, stocks and supplies and above all manpower. While the management information system should highlight many instances where resources are being used inefficiently (for example where staffing levels get out of line with current workloads) there is also a need for organisational procedures and controls over and above the use of such tools as performance measures. Examples of these procedures are set out below:

Manpower   Is there a procedure for 're-justifying' posts which become vacant at top management level? Does the organisation set up each year in its annual plan, operating goals, and work schedules which are carefully matched to manpower requirements by number, type and location?

Land and property   Is there a corporate procedure for identifying land and property surplus to specific requirements? Is the sale of the land processed expeditiously once identified? Who specifically is responsible for progressing the sale of the land? Are adequate marketing methods used for disposing of land and property? Is there a policy for identifying derelict and contaminated land and deciding on future use?

Experience shows that many public sector organisations have large areas of valuable surplus land which top management may be unaware of and which can tie up millions of pounds which could be better employed.

Energy   Have standards been set ie standard energy consumption for each building? Is there an energy conservation programme for all staff?

The public sector has perhaps been slow to invest money to obtain longer term savings in areas such as energy conservation. As an example of what can be achieved an energy review at the City of Birmingham identified savings of £1m per year through the introduction of electronic monitoring devices and tighter 'housekeeping'.

Current assets Are prompt billing and efficient recovery procedures in respect of sundry debtors (eg sundry housing debtors) observed? Is unnecessary cash tied up in stocks, is there scope for persuading suppliers to keep certain stocks? Are large amounts received by cheque/cash banked on the day of receipt?

Supplies and equipment Capital − is use made of discounted cash flow methods in assessing the benefits of capital cost saving schemes? Is the payback period realistic, say 2/3 years?
Revenue − are maximum discounts and the most beneficial prices obtained for items common across departments? An analysis carried out by the UK Audit Commission of prices paid by London Boroughs for identical items showed a range of prices which varied by as much as 130%.

Organisational Aspects

None of the procedures or systems used to achieve VFM will be successful if they are not backed by an effective organisational framework. As we have said, the investigation of VFM can be a sensitive area with, perhaps, 70% of savings relating to manpower costs. A strong commitment both from elected representatives and senior officials, is therefore required to ensure that possibly unpopular changes are implemented. Above all top management have to ensure a 'corporate' approach to value for money. Many managers fail to consider policy beyond areas affecting their own direct responsibilities. As a consequence, when 'belt tightening' takes place there is reluctance to share the burden.

In addition the corporate approach should allow liaison between departments to ensure that as much 'pooling' of facilities (eg transport, micro-computers etc) is carried out as possible. It is also important for pooling of skilled advice to take place. For example, vehicle acquisition should involve the user's requirements, the engineer's expertise in procurement of vehicles and planned maintenance and the finance officer's advice on funding and the economic life of the proposed acquisition.

The other fundamental organisational factor in achieving VFM is that the committee structure should be aligned with the management structure and the organisation's policies and services, otherwise it may not be possible to promote the appropriate degree of accountability and control.

The precise organisational structure to be adopted depends upon the nature of the public undertaking involved. In many local government organisations, elected members are extremely sensitive about the political implications of VFM reviews. Hence the degree of political activity in an organisation will have a bearing on their attitude towards performance reviews and the shape of the organisation. Furthermore, while it may be difficult for management to review objectively their own service it is equally difficult to persuade officers (even specialist management services units) from other departments to comment on sensitive matters relating to fellow officers' careers or empires.

With these factors in mind we believe that the normal review and monitoring process carried out by the service committees and their management should be overseen by a high level performance review committee with responsibility for directing and co-ordinating VFM reviews and most important, for implementing the recommendations arising.

Performance Review Committees

The Local Authorities Management Services and Computer Committee in the UK (LAMSAC) carried out a survey in local government which showed that 48% of councils had a formal performance review committee, 21% had formal performance review but no committee or sub-committee and 31% had no formal performance review arrangements. The survey also showed that councils with formal review arrangements generated about 18 VFM reports on average over the period surveyed compared to 0.8 for those with no formal review process.

This survey suggests that a formal performance review committee can provide the necessary impetus for VFM reviews. However, unless the Committee is small and powerful the reviews are likely to be superficial and sensitive recommendations will not be implemented. Ideally, in the case of say a local authority the Leader of the Council (that is the Leader of the controlling party) should chair the committee supported by chairmen of the major service committees.

The Chief Executive should also have a key role on the performance review committee because he acts as an essential link with the management team of chief officers. Normally, the management team, in liaison with service committees would submit projects for approval to the performance review committee who would draw up the rolling cost based review programme and decide priorities. Thereafter they would monitor the progress of the reviews and more particularly the implementation of the proposals in close liaison with the management team and the service committees.

The Review Teams

Only relatively large organisations would have the resources to justify a full-time management services unit to carry out cost based review work. The disadvantage of a full-time unit is that the staff are often reluctant to put forward recommendations affecting fellow officers' careers or other sensitive issues. They also often lack a sufficiently wide experience of other organisations and particularly of the private sector. In any event we believe it is useful for the service department under review to provide a seconded officer to the study team to ensure there is a full understanding of the ethos and culture of the service being studied. It is also necessary for the management unit to contain a nucleus of experienced specialists to ensure that sensitive work is carried out in a mature way. The unit should report either to the Chief Executive or directly to the responsible committee to ensure it is above interdepartmental rivalries.

An alternative to the use of a specialist VFM unit is to form working parties to review specific projects. Such working parties would report directly to the performance review committee. The working party may well make use of seconded specialists such as energy conservation officers or work study officers; it may even contain outside consultants. However, it should certainly contain one officer from the area under review.

Even in cases where the scale of operations would justify full time VFM practitioners, the public sector is generally not very good at investing in specialists (eg contract audit and energy conservation officers). Hence increasing use is being made of outside consultants who can draw on a wide range of specialists, provide an objective viewpoint from a diversity of experience and are not inhibited about drawing attention to sensitive issues. Considerable benefits can result when the consultant's work is closely monitored and co-ordinated by senior members and the consultants are given clear terms of reference. It is imperative however that only consultants with the sensitivity to appreciate the background and culture of government services should be used. Unfortunately many consultants do not understand fully the difference between the profit orientated approach of the private sector and the service-orientated approach in the public sector. Nevertheless, there is an increasing use made throughout the world of independent evaluators of VFM particularly in the field of programme effectiveness evaluation in central government departments and public utilities. This development has been encouraged in the USA by the requirement for each public sector programme to retain 1% of its budget for an evaluation of the programme's effectiveness.

Above all the organisation should ensure that chief officials are not merely good technicians but are good managers. There is a serious lack of basic management training for public sector officials, and many public authorities consider continuing management education as a wasteful overhead.

Incentives

Clearly, the motivation for achieving value for money has to come from the top. Top management's task can be made easier if there are incentives to offer operational management in return for their commitment. There is nothing more demoralising than for hard won savings to be made by one manager only to see the money spent by another. Whilst this situation may be unavoidable, the system should allow a manager the option of benefiting from at least part of any savings, by ploughing them back into investments which will bring about longer term savings or improvements (eg micro-computers, energy saving measures) transferring the savings to other cost centres (virement) or by carrying forward savings to the following year. There is also the question of adopting management and staff incentive schemes whereby officers could be paid a bonus for their success in meeting predetermined performance targets and other objectives and staff could be rewarded for worthwhile suggestions.

Incentive schemes are a little-explored area in the public sector and one that presents many traps for the unwary. Nevertheless, there are examples of their successful use and there is no doubt that if the right incentives are given then the independent VFM investigator will find that ideas will readily flow from management and staff.

APPENDIX   EXAMPLE OF SETTING LEVELS OF OBJECTIVES AND TARGETS (LONDON BOROUGH OF BEXLEY): HOUSING AND PERSONAL SERVICES COMMITTEE

Part I: Policy Objectives

A.   Strategic Plans

(i)   To formulate detailed proposals for the establishment of a mental health programme area within the Social Services Department.

(ii)   To determine the Housing Strategy and Investment Programme for 19XX.

(iii)   To formulate a strategy for Housing Association activity in Borough.

(iv)   To formulate plans for the ultimate development of the Preventative Division of the Environmental Health Department.

(v)   To formulate integrated Housing and Social Services Policies.

(vi)   To formulate a strategy to deal with the rising numbers of the over 75's.

(vii)   To develop a system of management audit of approved policies.

B.   Major Policy Objectives

(i)   To review the needs of the Under Fives and establish specific policies in relation to Day Nursery, Day Care and Child Minding Services.

(ii)   To commence work on the Review of the Needs of the Mentally Handicapped.

(iii)   To identify the resource implications of, and put forward proposals to implement, the Council's policies arising from the Review of the Needs of the Elderly and the Review of Residential, Domiciliary and Day Care Services for the Elderly.

(iv)   To establish and monitor the work of the Joint Care Planning Groups established by the Local Authority and the District Health Authority.

(v) To review the effectiveness and efficiency of Social Services Transport, and the Pest Control Service of the Environmental Health Department.

(vi) To take all necessary action arising out of the recommendations of the Social Services (Child Care Procedures) Panel.

(vii) To consider housing initiatives for first time buyers.

(viii) To plan co-ordinated action in the private housing sector and promote housing improvements.

(ix) To assist special needs groups such as the elderly.

C. Operational and Administrative Issues

(i) To implement the provisions of the Criminal Justice Act insofar as it relates to juveniles.

(ii) To implement the provisions of the Mental Health Amendment Act.

(iii) To review the Social Services In-service Training Programme in the light of the overall training strategy agreed by the Council.

(iv) To undertake an in-depth evaluation of the Council's Intermediate Treatment services.

Part II: Performance Standards/Targets

1. Social Services Department

			Anticipated workload	*Target performance*
(i)	Elderly			
	(a)	Bexley Residential Homes		
		Long stay places	405	96% occupancy
		Short stay places	32	75% occupancy by year end
	(b)	Day Care for Elderly		
		Places in Short stay Home	20	85% occupancy by year end
		Places in other Homes	12	85% occupancy
	(c)	No. of places in Agents Accommodation	40	95% occupancy
	(d)	No. of Meals on Wheels	168,376	98%
	(e)	Home Help Service hours	541,788	100%
(ii)	Child Care			
	(a)	Children in Care	270	100% of statutory reviews (every 6 months in required cases.)

		Anticipated workload	Target performance
(b)	Bexley Community Homes, places	30	85% occupancy
(c)	Children's Agents Accommodation		Not more than 63 places
(d)	Fostering Services:		
	Foster parents, No. available	68	100% by year end
	Children in Adolescent Fostering	5	100% by year end
(e)	Day Care and Supervision of Children		
	Intermediate Treatment, places	10	100%
	Day Nursery places for the Under 5's	45	85% occupancy
	Adoptions (Guardian ad Litem)	19	100%
	Child Abuse Service, Children on Register	130	100% (monitoring reviews)

Part III: Performances Standards/Targets

1. Finance Department

		Anticipated workload	Target performance
(i)	Closure of accounts 1982/83		By 31 July 1983
(ii)	Rate Collection: cost of collection		Staff costs to be less than 0.8% of cash collected. Rate arrears as a percentage of debit to be less than 4% at 30 September and less than 2% at 31 March.

		Anticipated workload	Target performance
(iii)	Housing Benefits	14,000	All applications received by 31 March to be determined prior to despatch of rate demand (90% + to be processed via the computer).
(iv)	Audit:		
	Resource allocation		
	Probity man days	2,063	
	Systems man days	1,187	
	Value for money man days	175	
		3,425	
	Other measures		90% of
	No. of establishments visited	200	programme
	No. of Audits completed:		
	Probity	250	
	Systems	100	
	Computer	171	
	Value for Money	15	
	No. of Contract System Reviews	14	
(v)	Insurance		
	Value of premiums paid	£357,000	Staff costs to be less than 5% of premiums paid. 100% to be passed to insurers within
	No. of claims	1,050	5 days of receipt.
(vi)	Payroll		
	Salaries: monthly paid	4,300	Staff costs to be less than 0.15% of pay bill.
	Pensions: weekly paid	480	Staff costs to be
	monthly paid	880	less than 0.04% of pay bill.
	Wages: weekly paid employees	4,000	Staff costs to be less than 1.4%
	Sessional and supply teachers etc. paid via		of pay bill.
	weekly payroll system	1,450	

4 Performance Measurement

Performance measurement is an important tool for evaluating value for money in the public sector. In the private sector detailed performance measurement is relatively less important because profitability tends to be used as the main overriding indicator. In the public sector the profit indicator is seldom available and the measurement of service outputs, particularly in areas such as social services, can be a difficult task especially in respect of effectiveness. After all, if the quality of a product in a commercial company is poor then the public will not buy it, which in turn affects profits. However, in the public sector the 'client' often has no alternative 'product' to use.

Measuring the performance of people and activities can have a number of different objectives. The results may be used for all or some of the following:

- determining that the benefits and impact looked for are being obtained
- getting assurance that goals are being met
- monitoring and controlling progress against plans
- justifying the use of resources
- assessing the overall effectiveness and efficiency of the activity
- providing a basis for calculating rewards and incentives
- to determine overall that value for money is being obtained.

In this chapter we study performance measures and how they are selected and calculated. We will consider the problems of setting standards both for quality and quantity. Finally we will illustrate how performance measurement systems are developed for the public sector and how the reports on performance and value for money can be presented.

Concepts we will be examining therefore are:

— measurement criteria and standards for value for money
— performance indicators to signpost value for money
— performance measurement systems for collecting and analysing value for money
— reporting methods to display value for money achievement.

How is Success Measured?

To be able to measure anything you need to know some very obvious things:

— exactly what is to be measured?
— what scale or 'yardstick' is to be used?
— the margin of error (tolerance) which can be allowed?
— who is to measure it?
— who is interested in the answer to the measurement and what will they do with these results?

For example, if you are measuring that a football ground conforms in size to the regulations, the process may be quite straightforward. The item to be measured is physical and fixed. The scale (metres or yards) is known and accepted. The tools are available and all you require is an assistant to hold the other end of the tape.

If however, you are measuring the success of a transport service the matters of why, what, and how are not as easily solved. Questions to be asked before measuring would include:

— what is the level or standard of service to be offered — regular, on demand or what?
— by whom is the success to be measured — the passengers, the authority organising the service, the organisation running the service or all of them?
— how is the profitability of the service to be assessed?
— how much weighting is to be given to such factors as reliability and impact on the morale of the community?

Measuring success in these circumstances is not just a matter of the number of miles travelled or the number of passengers carried. Although these quantified measures are important, the quality of the service is an equally important factor in such public sector organisations and getting value for money spent must consider both aspects.

Therefore, those responsible for setting the objectives of any function must decide on what criteria they intend to measure success and then develop from these criteria indicators which will tell them where to look for the signs of success or the lack of it.

Performance Indicators

Indicators point somewhere or at something. In the area of performance they should point at what is important to the success of what is being done. It may be possible to have one 'final performance indicator' or perhaps, five or six may be required to measure overall success. These are called High Level Performance Indicators. Below these, other indicators can be created to point at detailed achievements. As indicators become more accepted by an organisation they also become targets or goals at which the activity is aimed. So it is even more important to select and perfect the optimum set of performance indicators of any activity or organisation. Without agreed performance measures, those who are responsible for evaluating and perhaps for providing the funds, will use their own subjective judgement with an inevitable personal bias.

Selecting Performance Indicators

The first step in selecting appropriate performance indicators is to establish the objective of the activity or venture. Let us take an example from an agency concerned with providing funds for housing.

Housing Aid Agency

The objective of the agency is to provide funds for the construction of safe and sanitary homes for families in the lower-level income groups in the district.

As it presently stands, the objective statement gives to those involved in running the agency no real target to aim at, nor has the provider of funds any means of evaluating the results. Further, the families in the lower-level income group have no idea how many and how much will be provided. These three interested groups will each have their own view of what is an effective and efficient operation. The indicators selected for measuring must be sufficient in number and quality to meet the needs of the providers, the operators and the users of the service.

The objective of the agency requires some quantification or precision if it is to be used as the starting point for action and measurement:

- how many families are involved and how many do they intend to help?
- how does the agency intend to interpret safe, sanitary and lower-level income?
- what time-frame will it all take?
- how much can be achieved now and so on?

Answers to these questions will provide the basis for establishing the level of service we intend to provide. Measuring achievement can only be useful if the actual is compared to the possible and the possible has been defined in a plan capable of achievement. During a value for money assignment which we recently completed we measured the effectiveness of an international organisation who were providing famine relief in an African country. The organisation's resources could only provide for a small part of the total population needs. Our measures were established to assess how well they provided for that small group. The missing millions were outside the ability or power of the organisation to help and were outside the performance standards set. Ideal standards are rarely a good measure to use. The reasonably possible gives a fairer scale for judgement.

Let us now return to our agency and the provision of funds for housing. Here are eight possible indicators:

1) Number of families assisted
2) Amount of money allocated
3) Average time an application takes to be processed

4) Number of families on the waiting list
5) Number of complaints from families about the adequacy of funds
6) Number of complaints about the service of the agency
7) Number of complaints about the quality of the homes
8) Cost of running the agency.

Although this list looks complete and relevant it lacks:

— numbers (quantification)
— comparability (yardsticks)
— relationships (performance measures).

The indicators are shown, this time with numbers and comparisons, in Figure 4.1.

FIGURE 4.1   *Housing Aid Agency: Performance indicators and measures*

	For 3 months*	
Indicator	*Actual*	*Planned*
The number of families assisted	149	160
The amount of money allocated	£1,847,600	£1,920,000
The number of family applications still being processed	64	40
The average time an application takes to be processed	35 days	21 days
The number of complaints from families about:		
adequacy of funds	17	10
the service	14	10
the homes	11	10
The cost of running the agency	£16,092	£15,200

*3 months to 31 December 1984

When figure 4.1 is studied the picture becomes a little clearer but still can be improved upon. Hidden in all this are certain causes and effects which are important for performance and value for money evaluation.

By comparing and contrasting these indicators certain important measures can be calculated, highlighting efficiency, activity, economy and the acceptability of the service in the eyes of the users as shown in figure 4.2.

FIGURE **4.2**

Efficiency	Actual	Planned
In processing applications — Against planned $\dfrac{149}{160} \times 100$	93%	100%
Average time to process applications	35 days	21 days
Activity — Number of applications processed and in course of application, against planned $\dfrac{149 + 64}{160 + 40} \times 100$	106%	100%
Economy		
Average assistance per family	£12,400	£12,000
Average cost of applications processed and in process	£76	£76
Acceptability		
Complaints as percentage of applications processed:		
adequacy of funds	11.4%	6%
the service	9.4%	6%
the homes	7.4%	6%

In these figures you can see possible cause/effect factors which may be happening. For example, because the average processing time is 35 days as against 21 days a backlog of applications has built up (24) causing a certain number of complaints (14). The indicators and measures have identified a condition and two effects, now someone must find the cause. Perhaps the application forms are difficult to understand and complete, perhaps there was a postal strike, perhaps the agency staff are not yet organised.

In this example we have compared the actual performance with the planned or budgeted performance. We could have compared the actual with the performance for the preceding three months and obtained comparative information from that. Even better, if there are similar agencies in other districts a comparison of their performance indicators can highlight very useful information.

Some other aspects should be remembered in measuring performance:

— An organisation or function can only be measured for effectiveness of use of those resources allocated to it. In our example some higher authority decided that 160 families was the limit of those to be helped and that assistance needed or to be given (not the same thing) was £12,000. If there are another 300 families on a waiting list this figure is not taken into account in measuring the effectiveness of the agency. This would be a measure of the effectiveness of the higher authority in meeting wider needs.
— Information for measuring performance can come from within the organisation (internal measures) or from outside the organisation (external measures). Without appropriate external measures from customers, clients or competitors, an organisation has only half the picture, or at best, a photograph taken by itself. The same photograph taken by an outsider may have a totally different focus.
— Certain indicators can best be appreciated when viewed over a period of time where trends become clear. The use of index numbers is useful here.
— When measuring in terms of money spent, try and remove the effects of inflation to highlight the changes in real terms.

Those whose performance is being measured must also know on what basis it is being done and what weighting is to be given to the various qualities of performance. Those who are made responsible and accountable must be given some indication of what is expected from them.

Creating Performance Measurement Systems

Information to be of any value must be reliable, as accurate as necessary and available when required. To develop a performance measurement process requires us to consider the three stages of any system.

1) An input stage — having available relevant and accurate data.
2) A process stage — an activity by someone who collects and analyses the data into a logical and useful order to provide information.
3) An output stage — the production of reports and information for review and action.

In practice we find that many organisations have available almost all the data they require for value for money measures but do not have a systematic collection of it for this purpose. Data concerning money and purchases for example, are usually readily available within the accounting system and data about number of people served from other operating systems. New data is rarely required to be produced, what is needed is the re-arrangement of its order or its timing.

In this section we will illustrate how to design a value for money (performance measurement system) for three totally different types of activity.

1) *Administration*. The treasury section of a local authority whose objective is to collect income from rates.
2) *Leisure Services*. A library whose objective is to service the reading needs of a small town.
3) *Education and Welfare*. An organisation whose objective is to train blind people in skills which will help them to obtain work.

We will also illustrate a report format which would flow directly from these systems.

You, the reader, may not be involved directly in the design and running of such systems, only in the results. You should however, be aware of the various possible value for money indicators and how they are assembled.

To design a performance measurement system we must:

1) Decide what indicators are necessary to measure performance.
2) Make a list of the information needed to produce the indicators.
3) Break up this list into three sets:
    a) information that is already available
    b) information that is not yet available but the data exists and needs only to be collected together and analysed
    c) indicators where no information or data is available at the moment.
4) Decide how best to collect or create the missing data or information in (3) *b* or *c*. Important criteria here are:
    The amount of effort to collect it. It may be that some other departments are producing almost the same data for another purpose.
    The frequency with which it is needed — some activities need to be measured monthly, others annually, others on an ad-hoc basis.
    The accuracy required — remember that judgements on performance are rarely made to the last penny.
5) Now design the system — you have the input data and the output indicators. You will need to decide:
    The structure (keep it simple).
    Who is to do it.
    How often reports of performance will be required.

In our earlier example of the housing agency, the inputs were probably all available from other systems except perhaps for the complaints which may have required special lists to be kept. The task of analysis and of preparing a report would probably fall to the manager of the agency.

Let us now develop a system for performance measurement for the first of our three examples; the rates section of the treasury in a local authority.

Treasury — Collection of rates The key indicator for this clerical and administrative function is how quickly monies are collected when due. A secondary key measure is the costs of collection. To get value for money by improving effectiveness and efficiency we must speed up the collection and/or reduce the costs.

Data that will be required are:

cash collections and their timing
arrears — how much is outstanding and for how long?
cost of section or department
number of staff directly involved.

In this example all the data would be available from the accounting function. This performance measurement system will require little time to process and the report (see figure 4.3) could be completed promptly and at little cost. Adding the comparative figures and bringing these up to date is now a very simple process on a micro-computer.

From this report an elected member who may be less skilled in finance than in politics, can see quite quickly what has been achieved, any improvement from previous years and how well we are on target.

An additional column could have been introduced indicating the comparative figure of other authorities for this function. Such information is often available in the public sector. The competitive private sector is less generous with their figures.

The public library (Leisure services)   Developing a performance measurement system for a public library introduces some new problems:

— The staff of a library are not accountants and are thus less involved in collecting numerical data. On the other hand, they are systematic in approach.
— The needs and wants of the library users must constitute the major service goals of the library and any performance evaluation system must recognise this.
— There are costs of single units to be counted.
— Measuring quality as well as quantity is needed if the aspect of value as well as cost is to be appreciated.

The reader can visualise the likely inputs for the performance measurement system for a library. It has to do with books, users,

FIGURE 4.3 *Local Authority Performance Report*

Department – Treasury   *Activity* – Collection of Rate Income   *Date of report* –

Objective of Function – To collect from householders monies due in a prompt and economical manner

Indicators	This Month	Target	This Month Last Year
Effectiveness			
1 Performance of cash collection within:			
30 days	—	—	—
60 days	—	—	—
90 days	—	—	—
2 Accounts in arrears:			
Numbers	—	—	—
Percentage of total	—	—	—
Efficiency and Economy			
3 Workload – numbers of collections for staff employed	—	—	—
4 Cost per £1,000 of income collected	—	—	—

Remarks

Other ad-hoc effectiveness indicators will be used by reference to small random user surveys such as:

1 Accessibility of rates staff to answer enquiries from members of the public.
2 Format and presentation of rate returns to facilitate public understanding.

library staff and costs. The important thing is to decide which is important and significant and then to decide how easily it can be collected. Again we emphasise that the system must have the qualities of economy, simplicity and utility. Remember that any new system costs money to create and operate and must also be good value for money.

The main elements in evaluating a library may be summarised as follows:

Qualities	*Input Factors—Costs*	*Output Factors*
Activity	Issues of books and periodicals	Users
Efficiency	Library staff	
Economy	Facilities	
Effectiveness	Other supplies	

Considering the activity element for example, the objective is to maximise the activity of the library. Useful numbers to collect therefore would be daily users, books issued, enquiries answered, hours opened and so on.

However, activity does not mean value for money if the other three qualities are ignored. In the special performance report shown in Figure 4.4 we have matched all of the qualities with the factors involved and have produced performance indicators.

Certain of the indicators shown entail value judgements and are difficult to quantify or do not fit into the daily data collection. In service activities these are often the most important measures. Here are some for a public library.

- Appropriateness — is the library providing a balanced service for the needs of the users?
- Accessibility — is the library in the most suitable place and open at convenient hours?
- Awareness — do the users know where and what is available?
- Acceptability — are the users satisfied with the service they are receiving?

FIGURE 4.4 *Local Authority Performance Report*

Department – Leisure *Activity* – Libraries *Date of report* –

Indicators	This Quarter (Year)	Target	This Quarter Last Year	Average for 'Family' (where appropriate)
Economy and efficiency indicators				
1 Cost per 1,000 population for library services				
2 Ratio of library income to expenditure				
3 Number of book issues per hour per library assistant at branch libraries				
4 Cost per reference contact				
5 Cost per item catalogued per month				
6 Cost per unit of mobile library				
Effectiveness				
1 % of users that rate service as satisfactory (opening hours/ accessibility/choice)				
2 % reference questions answered satisfactorily				
3 % of households without valid membership				

These measures need data from outside the library in order to make useful VFM judgements. An appropriate sample of library users will therefore need to be interviewed using suitable questionnaires which are free of bias and unambiguous. Comparative information on libraries and their activities is widely available and used. With modern technology (eg micro-computers) a library can keep track of its own performance against similar institutions.

Vocational Training Scheme for the Blind (Education)   As we have seen, the design of VFM measurement indicators depends on the objective of the activity. The choice of indicator, the output of the system, should mirror what is important. In the two systems we have studied so far effectiveness and efficiency has been equally important. To improve effectiveness must not cost proportionally more time, effort and costs than is justified.

However, effectiveness (doing the right thing) supersedes efficiency in certain activities, famine or earthquake relief being a noteworthy example. This is probably also true of a training scheme for blind people. Economy may not be a suitable measure nor might hard efficiency numbers be the most appropriate 'High level' VFM indicator. While therefore economy and efficiency indicators have their place the emphasis in this type of activity should be on effectiveness in obtaining the results required by the policy makers.

Here are some significant results or success measures for a training programme.

Success Ratios
— Percentage of students completing the training.
— Percentage of students obtaining appropriate employment.
— Percentage of former students retaining employment after 12 months.

Satisfaction Ratios
— Percentage of former students indicating satisfaction with the training.
— Percentage of employers indicating satisfaction with the former students.

The data required to produce these ratios again needs special collection via surveys and questionnaires. Without it the input, ie number of students, costs, time spent will only tell us, at best, that we are doing things right, but not whether we are doing the right things. A specimen VFM report containing the performance indicators is shown as Figure 4.5

FIGURE 4.5   *EF Special Educational Services Performance (Value for Money) Report*

Department: Education

Activity: Training of Blind

Period: Six Months to October 19XX (Period 12)

Objective of Function

To provide functional training to blind citizens to enable them to find appropriate long-term employment.

Indicators	Period 12		Target		Period 11	
	No	%	No	%	No	%
Effectiveness/Success						
1 Students completing training Number/as percentage of starters	29	76	30	80	26	84
2 Number of students who obtain employment						
From Period 12 students	14	48	15	50	17	65
From Period 11 students (cumulative)	23	88	26	100	31	90
Average time before obtaining employment	11.5 weeks		8 weeks		10.4 weeks	
3 Satisfaction with training/survey						
Former students satisfied	13	93	15	100	15	88
Employers satisfied	14	100	14	100	30	95

FIGURE **4.5** *continued*

Indicators	Period 12 No	Period 12 %	Target No	Target %	Period 11 No	Period 11 %
4 Students withdrawing from training before completion	8	22	6	16	12	33
Efficiency and Economy						
5 Number of courses offered	6		8		6	
6 Student/teacher ratio	6.4/1		5/1		5.7/1	
7 Average class size per training course offered	8.1		6.0		7.2	
8 Costs						
Teaching costs	£26,800		£32,000		£25,400	
Other costs	£12,900		£14,000		£12,200	
Teaching costs per student course attended	£291		£296		£264	
Other costs per student course attended	£140		£130		£127	

Remarks

This report does not include all the possible indicators, only those that we decided were essential to this organisation's performance. Lower level indicators could be produced particularly if certain courses were either not in demand or costly to present.

Conclusion

In conclusion, it should be stressed that the use of performance measurement reports such as those shown in the foregoing examples, are not meant to form a management information system in their own right. They are meant to be an integrated part of the entire budgetary control, planning and review process for an authority. Indeed they can be regarded as the building blocks rather than the focal point of a comprehensive management reporting system. To illustrate this point figure 4.6 shows an

FIGURE 4.6 *Swimming Baths Activity Measure*

Usage of indoor pool	Forecast 1984/85	Anticipated 1983/84
Adult swimmers	45,000	45,000
Child swimmers	75,000	73,000
etc, etc.		

Key performance measures

Performance measure	Target	Last year
Economy and efficiency		
Cost per 1,000 swimmers	£x	£x
Cost per user taught to swim	£x	£x
Income as % of expenditure	x%	x%
% Use	x%	x%
Admin. and supervisory cost per user	£x	£x
Effectiveness		
Accident rate not exceeding	x%	x%
% small children taught to swim	x%	x%

Budget	Actual 1982/83	Budget 1983/84	Revised Budget 1983/84	Budget 1984/85	Variance 84/85-83/4
	£000	£000	£000	£000	£000
Employees					
Running Expenses					
Supplies and Services					
Transport and Plant					
Establishment Expenses					
Debt Charges					
Total Expenditure					
Income					
Net Expenditure					

example of a small district council's use of performance measures linked to a budget statement.

5 The Social Consequences of Value for Money

'The moment a squeeze on numbers is necessary it is not the layers of fat that disappear. It is those at the sharp end that tend to suffer.'

Sir Derek Rayner

Many politicians are concerned that a major consequence of VFM reviews is to identify instances of overstaffing. This is understandable, bearing in mind that 60–70% of public sector costs are concerned with people ie salaries, wages, employment oncosts etc. To correct these situations may at first sight appear to necessitate some redundancies. In many countries there are serious problems of underemployment so that redundancy or even the reduction of existing employment levels by other means is politically undesirable. Many countries have employment legislation which rules out forced redundancy. These serious concerns may lead politicians and public servants to believe that value for money reviews are a waste of time. This is not correct because reviews are not intended solely to identify opportunities for reducing staff numbers. Value for money reviews are concerned with identifying wasteful and ineffective use of resources, be they people, cash or property.

In most countries public money is derived at a national level from a range of sources and there is little clear definition of the purposes for which it is obtained other than the general intention to fund public expenditure. Some countries levy taxes which are stated to be intended for specific purposes but this is rare and the purposes are seldom expressed as exclusive. At a local level however, it is much more common for taxes to be levied on a basis which includes specific declarations as to the intended uses for the funds. Also that part of local expenditure which is covered by allocations from central government is commonly funded on a basis which involves at least a general declaration of the intended purposes for the money.

In these circumstances the diversion of funds for purposes which have not been declared is at the least a breach of trust and may even be considered to be a fraud upon the taxpayers. It is of more serious social and moral consequence if funds declared, for example, as being intended for the care of the mentally ill are diverted to other purposes. This is tantamount to robbing a largely defenceless section of the community of some part of the standard of care to which it is entitled and which the taxpayers were led to believe it would receive.

The maintenance of avoidably high levels of staffing in sections of the public service is a diversion of funds from the purposes for which they were intended unless, and only unless, the full cost of the extra staff is fully met from funds specifically declared for use in maintaining employment levels.

No sensible or sensitive person would question that the maintenance of existing levels of employment and indeed the reduction of the numbers unemployed are both desirable and meritorious objectives. The argument is solely against deceit and deception in funding these objectives. If the objectives are funded from monies clearly stated to be levied or allocated for the purpose there can be no objection. The normal checks and balances in the legal, legislative and democratic systems in the country concerned can operate freely.

If, however, the objectives are met by using funds declared for other purposes the practice should be condemned.

There is a further aspect to this problem which receives too little consideration from those involved in the management of the public sector. Contrary to popular myth the majority of public servants are sincere, conscientious people, motivated by the same desires and satisfactions as other members of the working population. Given the opportunity they will work willingly and hard. They like to take pride in their work and to feel that they make a valuable and full contribution to the community.

Public servants are also usually the first to be aware if they are used unproductively on wasteful and unnecessary activities. It follows that overstaffing will lead to poor staff morale and in the long term to a steady deterioration in the quality of staff retained in the public sector as the more able members leave for more satisfying and challenging occupations.

What then can the decision maker do to solve the problems of overstaffing? There are a number of solutions which involve the planning of staff reductions over a period so as to take full advantage of the opportunities for genuine redeployment combined with natural wastage, voluntary redundancy and early retirement. The best solution in any particular case will depend on the precise terms of employment of staff and the legislative constraints in the country. However, all these solutions share one common disadvantage; there is a reduction in the future employment opportunities.

There is one possible solution to the problem of overstaffing which does not involve a reduction in future employment opportunities and which can avoid the use of voluntary redundancy, natural wastage and early retirement. This solution involves examining the basis on which one determines that overstaffing exists.

Overstaffing is a situation in which the number of staff employed on a task exceeds the minimum number required to carry out that task on a continuing basis and to an acceptable standard of service. If this definition is accepted it is clear that there is considerable scope for variation in two areas. Firstly in the standard of service which is considered acceptable and secondly in the scope of the task which a group of staff is called upon to carry out. To put it very simply one can increase the service to the public so as to take up the slack in the staffing.

The increased service can be manifested either as an increase in the quality of an existing service or in the provision of a new service. Provided the increased service is useful and of genuine benefit to the public there can be no real complaint at the use of existing public resources to provide it.

The message of this chapter is that value for money auditing is not a tool for reducing staffing levels, an axe to be wielded by the cost cutters. Value for money is concerned with identifying wasteful and ineffective use of resources so that these resources can be made available for more productive use. It is for the politician to decide whether that more productive use is to be found by retaining the resources in the public sector or by returning them to the taxpayer.

Part II Methods and Techniques

6 Organising and Carrying Out Reviews

'Value for money (VFM) auditing depends on the application of common sense. A successful VFM auditor needs to be constructively sceptical, to have a sense of humour and a sense of the significant. The scepticism is necessary to question existing progress. The sense of humour will help him to get on well with the people he is auditing. . .the sense of the significant is essential as his time is limited.'

John Redwood
All Souls College, Oxford

An essential element of good value for money practice is the systematic review of operations with the intention of improving economy or efficiency and making services more effective. To this end each organisation should establish a rolling review process which examines critically and objectively each main activity over a period of say four or five years. The broad scope of such reviews falls naturally into two parts:

1) Cost based reviews (economy and efficiency)
2) The evaluation of management's success in meeting policy objectives (effectiveness).

Furthermore, it will be necessary to review economy, efficiency and effectiveness on two separate levels whether the review is directed at individual departments, functions, programmes or activities. Firstly, the review will seek to identify significant saving and improvements in the efficiency and effectiveness of services. Secondly, the review will have the longer term objective of improving management's control over the economy, efficiency and effectiveness of the activities for which they are responsible in terms of such aspects as performance measurement. Also, before an organisation's self assessment process begins it will be important to have regard to a number of factors, which if not observed will quickly bring the process into disrepute.

Above all it is necessary to choose mature and experienced people to carry out this most delicate work, the outcome of which may have a profound effect on the careers of management and staff.

It is also essential for the review staff to be supported by top management otherwise the value for money reports will merely gather dust on someone's shelf. Furthermore value for money projects must be carefully selected and planned if scarce resources are not to be wasted in reviewing areas which offer little or no chance of 'payback'. The reviews themselves need to be carried out in a structured and well co-ordinated manner and have regard to the latest 'state of the art' in terms of methodology and techniques.

At the same time work plans must be flexible and allow for interesting detours, the work demands a high degree of initiative and original thought, it has no place for junior staff slavishly working through checklists. Finally, the work demands sensitive and sympathetic liaison and discussion arrangements with all affected by the review: politicians, management, staff and unions. Reports should not be presented as *fait accompli* and should give praise as well as criticism. Each of these aspects is examined in more detail in the remainder of this chapter.

Types of Review

First, a word about the balance to be struck between the review of economy and efficiency on the one hand and effectiveness on the other. No one should doubt that every review should cover all aspects, after all there is no point in carrying out activities economically and efficiently if they are providing the wrong type or level of service. However, in the past value for money reviews in the main have concentrated upon economy and efficiency. For one thing, these areas are easier to tackle whereas the techniques for reviewing effectiveness are relatively in their infancy. For another, management in the public sector is invariably preoccupied with the immediate need to save costs.

In recognition of management's need to contain costs we have devoted a significant part of this book to methods which might be used to achieve cost reductions. For example, Chapter 7 deals exclusively with ways of combating waste while Chapter 10 examines opportunities for saving money through contracting out services to the private sector.

While we have not neglected the effectiveness aspect of public sector services we have to accept that although well tried methods for improving economy and efficiency can be applied to any type of public sector activity, the evaluation of effectiveness is a much more diverse and complex area which defies a completely stand-ardised approach. There is a world of difference between evaluating the effectiveness of, say, the maintenance division of an education authority and that of the Concorde project. While the former provides easily definable and measurable objectives, the latter's objectives are much more obscure with intangibles such as national prestige entering the reckoning.

We have therefore based our approach to effectiveness review in this chapter at the level of relatively straightforward pro-grammes which provide manageable evaluations. Having said that, we recognise that much more sophisticated methodology is available for evaluating the effectiveness of very large complex national programmes such as, for example, programme evalu-ation techniques.

Selecting the Project

The sheer size and diversity of public sector work requires that value for money projects are carefully selected to ensure that only areas offering significant potential for improvement are reviewed, otherwise scarce manpower resources will be frittered away in reviewing activities where there is little prospect of finding anything worthwhile.

A reasonably scientific but flexible, approach is required to gradually 'refine' the broad areas initially selected for review to the point where discrete, manageable and fruitful projects are identified for in-depth investigation.

In selecting the initial broad areas for review, management should be guided by a number of factors. It is important that areas of substantial spending are identified by reference to the budget. Generally, we should not concern ourselves with areas of low cost. However we should not ignore the possibility of 'across the board' reviews of say purchasing or telephone costs, where the cost broken down by department is relatively small, but the overall cost to the organisation is significant.

In terms of a local authority, for example, the Education department may be selected as the first priority for review on the grounds of its high cost. However, it would not be sensible to allow the review team 'carte blanche' to investigate the entire Education department; such an undertaking might take many man-years to complete with little benefit being derived from many areas. Management may consider that the greatest benefit would be derived from concentrating on 'non-teaching' costs such as cleaning, energy and administrative and technical staff which in a typical Metropolitan Borough, might account for £20 million per year.

Once the broad areas for review have been identified, a strategic review plan would be agreed for a period of say four to five years. Priorities for reviewing the areas included in the plan would be prioritised on the basis of a number of factors including:

1) Materiality. (For guidance a schedule setting out common key expense headings in the public sector prepared by CIPFA is shown in Appendix I to this chapter).
2) Known problems (eg excessive housing rent arrears).
3) National initiatives such as the studies carried out by the Audit Commission for Local Government in England and Wales in areas such as vehicle maintenance, children in care and central purchasing and stores. Other well known initiatives in the UK include those carried out by the National Health Service through 'Rayner' type studies into such areas as non-ambulance transport and prescription costs.
4) Examples of successful reviews in other organisations (eg contracting out of refuse collection).

The advantage of initially selecting a project which has success-fully provided significant improvements in another organisation is that it clearly increases the chances of achieving an early success in the review programme. The need to gain credibility for the review team at the outset is very important. In this regard, we have highlighted in Chapter 7 (Combating Waste) a number of areas in the public sector which consistently provide scope for saving or improvement.

Once the strategic plan identifying broad areas for review has been agreed, the review team, in liaison with management, will gradually narrow down each project to a more manageable and fruitful area. Initially this can be achieved by further 'desk' research into successful studies carried out in other organisations, by reference for example to the CIPFA 'Value for Money Handbook' which provides a wide range of VFM case studies. Potential areas for improvement can also be found in budget statements and financial accounts to identify interesting trends such as, for example, increases in the ratio of administrative costs to fieldworkers in a Social Services department.

Similarly broad comparisons of performance can be made by reference to published statistics including the CIPFA comparative costs and performance indicators and the Audit Commission's 'profiles' which highlight instances where an Authority's spending for a particular cost element deviates significantly from the average for the 'family' or 'cluster' or similar authorities. An extract from the 'profile' is shown in figure 6.1. The cluster analysis has been a significant development in comparative statistics because it seeks to group together for comparative purposes authorities who have similar characteristics, such as age profiles, unemployment rates, number of shared dwellings and amount of agricultural land.

Even though such techniques as the 'cluster' analysis help us to compare 'like with like'. Such comparisons need to be treated with great care. As we indicated earlier, statistics such as these only pose questions, they do not provide answers. It may not be possible at this stage for example to differentiate between planned high spending as a policy decision (for instance in the provision of a larger area of open recreation space than recommended by the UK National Playing Fields Association), and inefficient spending (for instance in excessively high maintenance costs per hectare for recreation areas due to overmanning). Nonetheless,

Education (1)   SERVICE STATISTICS

Primary Schools

| | This LA | ------Family------ | | | Difference from average £000 |
		Low	Average	High	
Pupil/teacher ratio	22.0	20.6	21.9	23.7	
Pupils per school	167	119	170	242	
Expenditure/income per pupil:					
Teaching staff	456	443	473	502	511
Support staff	7	7	26	42	
Premises related staff	32	32	42	51	
Admin & clerical staff	21	5	10	21	
Repairs & maintenance	33	33	45	80	
Fuel & light	30	27	35	41	
Books & equipment	20	18	23	33	
Transport	8	4	9	25	
Other expenditure	25	25	35	53	
Gross expenditure	632	627	698	760	
Income from other LEAs	1	1	2	9	
Other income	2	1	2	5	
Net expenditure	629	624	694	756	
Teaching cost per teacher	10,017	9,928	10,337	11,166	

FIGURE 6.1 *Service Statistics*

Secondary Schools

	This LA	Low	Family Average	High	Difference from average £000
Pupil/teacher ratio	16.7	15.3	16.6	17.5	
Pupils per school	758	487	836	1,111	
Expenditure/income per pupil:					
Teaching staff	635	619	648	709	
Support staff	17	10	20	30	
Premises related staff	42	36	45	56	
Admin & clerical staff	16	9	16	26	
Repairs & maintenance	39	34	46	62	
Fuel & light	42	36	43	53	
Books & equipment	38	28	38	48	
Transport	37	8	35	74	
Other expenditure	65	58	82	122	
Gross expenditure	932	907	973	1,127	
Income from other LEAs	2	2	8	23	
Other income	6	1	4	7	
Net expenditure	923	888	962	1,123	
Teaching cost per teacher	10,439	10,415	10,683	10,977	

FIGURE 6.1 *Service Statistics (cont.)*

the use of comparative performance measures such as education cost per pupil will at least direct attention to potential areas for improvement.

By this stage, therefore, our initial project may have been refined further to say a review of non-teaching costs for the central services section of the Education department, larger secondary schools and colleges of further education.

Pilot Studies

It is suggested that the final 'refining' process is best carried out by means of a brief 'pilot study'. A pilot study, lasting perhaps up to a week depending upon the size and complexity of the activity, will have the purpose of identifying specific areas for detailed review within the broad area originally selected. During the course of the study the review team would expect to carry out the following tasks.

1) Interview key officers in the department.
2) Gain a more detailed insight into the policy objectives for the area under review, ascertain how the success of these policy objectives is measured and how the management measures efficiency (productivity indicators etc).
3) Obtain broad staffing levels, the mix and relationship of staff levels to activity over the past three to four years.
4) Get copies of organisation charts and job descriptions.
5) Ascertain officials' own ideas for improvement. Often these can be worthwhile but may not have found favour with politicians or senior management for a variety of reasons.
6) Carry out more detailed cost and statistical comparisons.

At the end of this brief review a number of promising areas should have been identified for detailed review. It must be borne in mind however that the pilot study is concerned primarily with isolating areas for the detailed programme of work. Certainly it would not be possible to reach any firm conclusions at this stage.

At the end of the pilot study therefore, it will be possible to draw up firm terms of reference and a work programme for agreement with top management. At this stage our Education project may for example have been narrowed down to a review of administrative and technical support staff and cleaning and energy costs for secondary schools and colleges of further education. However, it should be stressed that while a structured programme of work is important it should be flexible. Value for money work requires open-mindedness and the ability to change direction if a more promising area of research presents itself.

Approach to the Detailed Review

As we have stressed earlier, successful value for money reviews rely upon a fresh and inventive approach which could be inhibited by too many rules. Furthermore, while this work demands the use of certain formal techniques such as performance measurement, successful value for money studies owe as much to the sensitive and sympathetic way in which people are handled as to formal methodology.

Nevertheless, value for money reviews do lend themselves naturally to a structured approach which falls under three main headings:

1) *Input based reviews* − this approach largely consists of statistical analysis and comparisons including the use of performance measurement to evaluate economy and efficiency. The potential areas identified for improvement in this review lead into the more detailed 'systems based' review.
2) *Systems based review* − this covers a review of staffing levels, organisational structure, activity levels and procedures and is designed to uncover the root cause of problems identified in (1) above. For example, the statistical analysis may have highlighted that the turnround time on planning applications for an authority is longer than the national average. The systems review would be necessary to uncover the fact that there were bottlenecks in the procedures or perhaps that certain staff were not properly qualified to do the work.
3) *Output based review* − a review of policy objectives, the activities required to achieve the objectives and the use of performance measures to assess the effectiveness of policies.

The first two types of review therefore are concerned primarily with the questions 'can cost be reduced for the same output?' and 'can greater output be achieved for the same cost?'. The output based review relates to performance in achieving policy goals or objectives and, to a large extent, the ability to do this depends upon the clarity with which these objectives are stated. Where there is no clear understanding of policy by elected representatives or officers then clearly there is a serious lack of control present in the organisation.

Input Based Review

The starting point therefore for an economy and efficiency review is an analysis of costs or income in relation to output (eg cost of rent or rate collection per 1,000 householders, cost per ton of refuse collected), in other words the use of performance measurement techniques.

The subject of performance measurement has been explored in detail earlier, but it is worth repeating that performance measurement is only of value if suitable yardsticks are used to compare the authority's performance. In this respect a number of sources should be used, both external and internal. For example, in a recent review of a water authority's clerical productivity, comparisons were made not only with past periods and between divisions within the authority, but with other water authorities and also private sector organisations.

It should be emphasised however, that comparisons with outside sources, even with local authorities of similar demographic and economic background, need to be treated with caution. Often the basis for the computation of costs may be different, for example the extent to which central overheads such as computer costs are included. More importantly, high costs in a particular area may be indicative not of inefficiency but of the provision of high service levels, which is a policy matter. Above all, analysis by performance measure is not an end in itself. It is merely the tool with which we identify potentially weak areas. In order to find the underlying cause of these weaknesses we must review procedures and staffing levels, ie use the 'systems based' approach described below.

Despite these reservations about comparative analysis however, we believe it is a valuable management tool in the evaluation of VFM. It is especially useful when a 'top down' review is made whereby an initial overview of costs is made to identify potential areas of high cost or inefficiency. For example, the review of a finance department may reveal that the total costs per 1,000 population in the authority are high compared to other similar authorities and are on a rising trend. Successively therefore unit costs and productivity would be compared at lower levels until specific areas of potential overspending were found. In the finance department therefore our initial comparison might lead us to make similar comparisons for the main sections within finance, say computers, rates, accounting and establishment. Assuming perhaps that our investigations lead us to the conclusion that the costs of the rates section were high we might proceed to carry out the following further comparisons:

1) Rate collection costs per 1,000 ratepayers: other authorities
2) % arrears: other authorities
3) Rate collection costs section by section per 1,000 ratepayers: previous periods
4) Number of rebates processed per clerk per week: previous periods.

This is a technique well tried in commerce, as exemplified by the UK Centre for Interfirm Comparisons. A similar technique has been developed by the UK Audit Commission called 'logic trees' which has the added feature of readily differentiating between high costs potentially caused by inefficiency and high costs attributable to policy decisions. The use of 'logic trees' is illustrated in Figure 6.2.

Systems Based Review

The areas for further review identified by the input based review or cost analysis phase would therefore be followed up in the 'systems based' review phase. In this regard, there is a well defined methodology for dealing with systems based reviews in terms of such techniques as interviewing, activity sampling and

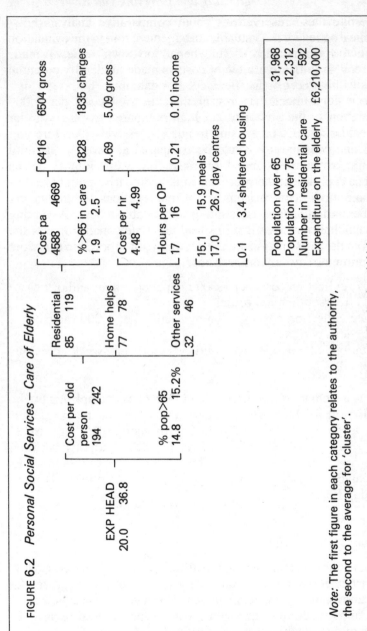

FIGURE 6.2 *Personal Social Services – Care of Elderly*

EXP HEAD
20.0   36.8

Cost per old person
194   242

% pop>65
14.8   15.2%

Residential
85   119

Cost pa
4588   4669   6416   6504 gross

%>65 in care
1.9   2.5   1828   1835 charges

Home helps
77   78

Cost per hr
4.48   4.99   4.69   5.09 gross

Hours per OP
17   16   0.21   0.10 income

Other services
32   46

15.1   15.9 meals
17.0   26.7 day centres

0.1   3.4 sheltered housing

Population over 65	31,968
Population over 75	12,312
Number in residential care	592
Expenditure on the elderly	£6,210,000

Note: The first figure in each category relates to the authority, the second to the average for 'cluster'.

Source: Audit Commission for Local Government in England and Wales.

organisation and methods studies. These techniques are applicable to both the private and the public sector and this book is not the place to deal with methods which are of more interest to the VFM practitioner than to management. There are many detailed works on the subject including the Price Waterhouse 'Value for Money Auditing Manual' published by Gee & Co. However, the main techniques used for this phase of the review would be:

1) *Examining existing records* − eg management accounts and budgets, returns and work files.

2) *Written questionnaires* − the use of questionnaires as 'aide-mémoires' for experienced investigators is encouraged. These are particularly useful for 'across the board' studies such as vehicle utilisation. Examples of key point checklists are to be found in Chapter 12. More detailed questionnaires on key review areas such as energy, purchases, manpower and new technology are to be found in the Price Waterhouse Value for Money Auditing Manual.

3) *Interviews and informal discussion* − with politicians, management and staff in the areas under review.

4) *Direct observation* − or where appropriate, by such techniques as activity sampling (ie measuring and comparing the output and productivity of selected staff or units).

By a combination of these methods the main aims of the detailed review would be to establish:

1) What are the activities for each area under review, how is their economy and efficiency measured and what corrective action is taken?

2) Do the systems and the organisational structure provide the right background and information to allow a proper control to be exercised over its resources?

3) About each activity under review 'why is the work done?' and if it has to be done 'why is it done as it is?'

4) How are the pricing policies calculated, how often are they reviewed and is the marketing of such services as leisure centres carried out in a professional way?

5) Can costs be reduced or the work be carried out more cheaply outside without impairing services?

6) What would be the effect of changing standards or service levels (eg reference facilities at libraries, buffer stocks of spare parts)?

These questions about economy and efficiency can probably be answered without too much difficulty given that the investigators have an open-minded and commonsense approach.

Output Based Review

As we have indicated, however, the review of effectiveness is much more difficult to carry out. The problem lies in the precise definition of policy objectives. These are not always cohesive or compatible with each other, as many of the different views that are held on a wide range of activities are often political. Even where it is possible to define the objectives of a policy clearly there are instances where it is very difficult if not impossible to evaluate the success of a particular policy. Richard Brown in his book 'Auditing Performance in Government' says:

. . .many programs may not lend themselves to definitive measurement of results. For example should the success of an alcoholism program be measured by using the numbers of patients whose consumption is reduced? How, if at all, can the program's impact be segregated from other social factors which may affect their consumption?

Because of the difficulties therefore in evaluating the effectiveness of policies it is suggested that reviews in this area should be carried out at a senior level. However, even though the investigators should operate at a high level, they should concern themselves only with evaluating the outcomes of policies not with the appropriateness of the policies themselves, unless they are specifically asked to do so. For example, a policy objective for a municipal highways department is to relieve traffic congestion. Tangible outcomes of this policy could be found in programmes to introduce one-way traffic systems, bus lanes etc. It is the investigator's job to evaluate whether these programmes are successful and if they are not, to suggest that alternative strategies be studied and introduced.

In practical terms therefore, bearing in mind time constraints and the political nature of the work, the reviewer of effectiveness will not go so far in recommending solutions as will the reviewer of economy and efficiency. Indeed, the principal concern of the evaluator of effectiveness will be to decide whether or not management themselves have adequate methods for measuring the effectiveness of activities and programmes on an ongoing basis.

In carrying out an effectiveness (or output based) review therefore we are concerned mainly to:

1) Establish whether for the policy area under review the organisation has:
   a) set reasonably well defined objectives
   b) communicated these clearly to management and staff
   c) established yardsticks with which to measure the effectiveness of its programmes for achieving policy objectives
   d) adequate reporting systems
   e) taken appropriate corrective action where necessary.
2) Ascertain whether management regularly considers the incremental effects of changing service levels (eg maintenance periods) or the effects of introducing alternative programmes (eg transferring children in care from residential homes to foster homes).

Providing therefore that proper evaluation systems are in place, that they appear to be accurate and that management are acting upon them, the investigator can be satisfied. However, in practice adequate measurement systems will not always exist and the investigator in these circumstances will need to carry out his own 'ad-hoc' tests on the outcome of programmes, using performance measures designed by himself, in order to test whether policy objectives have been met.

We gave the example in an earlier chapter of a vocational training programme for the blind. The department may use as a simple measure the percentage of graduates from the course who gain employment. However, this alone is not a true measure of the programme's effectiveness. Three items remain to be checked by the reviewer:

1) Does the employment relate to the training received (eg telephonist not dishwasher)?

2) What is the average length of time such training related employment is retained?
3) How does the success of the programme in terms of placement rate and retention compare with accepted standards or similar programmes, perhaps in other countries?

Evaluation may not always be so easy as in this particular example, where reasonably accessible measures exist. In practice, quantitative measures are not always available. Often the only means of assessing effectiveness is to ask a sample of users for their opinion of the service they have received. Clearly even this approach is not appropriate for all situations, as for example in the case of nursery school students. Nevertheless, it does provide a means of ascertaining directly the views of the taxpayer and ratepayer.

User surveys are a technique which has been used extensively in the USA and Canada in such areas as social services, street cleansing, police, fire services and leisure services. Indeed an organisation called the Dayton Public Opinion Center has been set up in Ohio for the specific purpose of carrying out 'citizen surveys' for municipalities. While this technique is extremely useful it nonetheless requires great care in its application and it is not cheap to use. In particular, considerable thought has to be given to sample sizes and to designing bias free questionnaires.

Our suggested approach to evaluating effectiveness is summarised in step by step form in Figure 6.3.

Relations with Staff

Before any review commences, its terms of reference should be discussed and agreed by the review team with the departmental head of the area under review. This officer in turn should notify the staff (and the unions when appropriate) of the purpose and scope of the work in order to clear up any misconceptions about the review. Also, at an early stage, separate meetings should be held with management and with staff associations or union representatives to agree the reporting back arrangements. This 'set-up'

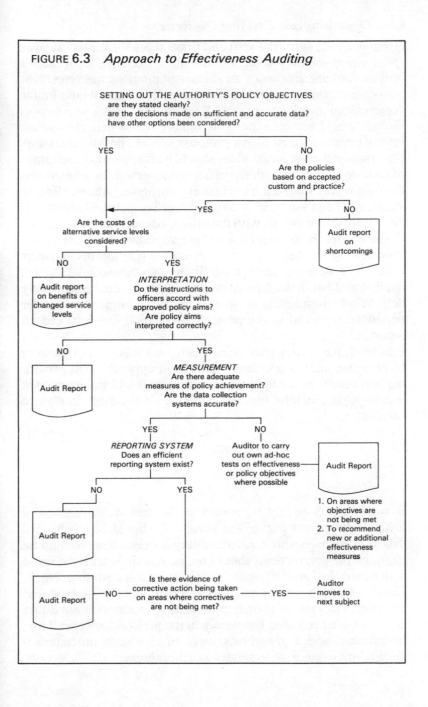

FIGURE 6.3 *Approach to Effectiveness Auditing*

SETTING OUT THE AUTHORITY'S POLICY OBJECTIVES
are they stated clearly?
are the decisions made on sufficient and accurate data?
have other options been considered?

YES   NO
                                       Are the policies
                                       based on accepted
                                       custom and practice?

                    YES   NO

Are the costs of   Audit report
alternative service levels   on
considered?   shortcomings

NO   YES

Audit report   *INTERPRETATION*
on benefits of Do the instructions to
changed service officers accord with
levels   approved policy aims?
                Are policy aims
                interpreted correctly?

NO   YES

Audit Report   *MEASUREMENT*
                Are there adequate
                measures of policy achievement?
                Are the data collection
                systems accurate?

        YES   NO

REPORTING SYSTEM   Auditor to carry
Does an efficient   out own ad-hoc
reporting system exist? tests on effectiveness   Audit Report
                        or policy objectives
                        where possible

NO   YES   1. On areas where
                                                    objectives are
                                                    not being met
Audit Report   2. To recommend
                                                    new or additional
                                                    effectiveness
                                                    measures

                Is there evidence of   Auditor
Audit Report —NO— corrective action being taken moves to
                on areas where correctives —YES— next subject
                are not being met?

meeting should agree the start and finish dates for the work, what specific help the review team will require from the department's staff and also the frequency and nature of progress meetings.

Normally, the main contact for the review team would be the departmental head concerned. Regular, say weekly meetings should be held between the head and the senior officers and the review team to discuss ideas, progress and any problems arising. On a more informal basis, ideas should be discussed at each stage of their development with the officers concerned. In other words the final report should not contain any surprises. Above all ideas should not be put in writing to an officer's superior without first discussing the proposals with the officer concerned.

The approach to interviewing management and staff is all-important to the success of the review. While the review team have to be determined and persistent they should not appear inquisitorial but make it clear they are there to offer constructive help. Where useful ideas are gained from staff or management the review team should where possible give credit for them in their report.

In brief, the review team should carry out their work in a spirit of openness and co-operation. This joint approach will provide the best results in the long term, indeed staff will go out of their way to provide helpful ideas with the reviewer acting simply as a catalyst.

Trade Unions

It would not normally be necessary to deal with trade union officials directly as part of the review. It should be emphasised that it is management's responsibility to deal with the unions although the review team should attend meetings with the union officials, if, and only if, senior officials feel it is desirable. On the occasions where regular progress meetings are necessary it may be helpful to agree a formal consultation procedure. Such procedures have been used frequently in the past on our consultancy assignments and a general example of one such procedure is shown for guidance in Appendix 2 to this chapter.

Reporting

The style and layout of the final report is a matter of personal choice for the writer and is not a matter for discussion here. However, the guiding spirit behind the preparation of a VFM report is that the purpose of a review is not merely to gather facts but to initiate action for improvement. The report should be practical in nature and offer solutions, not merely identify problems.

The report should be suitably succinct for busy officials to read and should contain a brief key point management summary at the beginning. The liberal use of graphs and pictures is often the best method of explaining the facts. As mentioned earlier, it is important for draft reports to be cleared with each level of management concerned before the final report is submitted.

The report should therefore be regarded as an aid to management in the efficient and effective use of resources and not as a catalogue of deficiencies. On the occasions where the department or activity is operating efficiently this must be acknowledged as it is essential that a balanced report should be presented which will form a constructive guide and stimulus to management. It is important to avoid using forms of words which might antagonise or stimulate a defensive attitude and the report should also recognise any constraining factors operating on management which may have prevented them from action in the past.

The precise contents of each report will vary materially depending on the size and nature of the problem; however, the report would invariably discuss the following matters:

Economy and Efficiency

1) Opportunities to improve management's control over the achievement of value for money eg in the recommendation of key performance measures for monitoring the ongoing productivity of activities.
2) Opportunities to reduce costs without impairing service levels or to increase output at no extra cost by changing operations or staffing levels.
3) Opportunities to beneficially contract out certain services.

4) Areas where further review is required to evaluate potential savings.
5) An action plan.

Effectiveness

1) Whether policy objectives are stated clearly and whether the programmes designed to achieve them are a fair representation of these objectives.
2) Whether sufficient guidance is given to management on how to achieve policy objectives.
3) The extent to which goals are being achieved.
4) Opportunities to improve the way in which the department measures and reports the success or otherwise of its programmes.
5) Steps to be taken to implement the changes needed to ensure programmes achieve the desired objectives (where possible).
6) Comments on the validity of the policy itself (if top management ask the review team for such comments).

The VFM report represents material evidence of the quality of the reviewer's work. The reputation for good work will spread quickly but news of poor work will spread even more quickly in the enclosed world of the public sector, whether at central or local level. It is important therefore to produce high quality and action based reports.

Control of Reviews

As we have repeatedly stated, significant improvements will not be achieved unless there is determined support from top management for VFM projects. Regardless of the type of public sector organisation involved there should be control over the VFM work by a high-level committee who are above inter-departmental rivalries and vested interests and who have the power to take perhaps unpopular and radical decisions.

Ideally, such a committee should have a balance of senior management and elected representatives (or co-opted lay members) in order to provide an objective and powerful direction for the reviews. At local government level the group would probably be a sub-committee of the policy and resources committee and would typically be called the performance review committee. The constitution of such a committee would be:

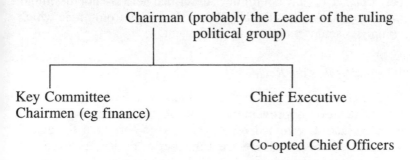

Chairman (probably the Leader of the ruling political group)

Key Committee Chairmen (eg finance)

Chief Executive

Co-opted Chief Officers

Thus the committee should be powerful but small in number (not more than 8) and work closely with the management team of Chief Officers through the Chief Executive. The management team would in turn liaise closely with service committee chairmen in such matters as the selection of subjects for review.

The function of the performance review committee would be as follows:

1) Agree (following recommendations from the management team and service committee chairmen) a rolling review programme.
2) Agree terms of reference for each project.
3) Monitor progress on on-going reviews and receive interim reports.
4) Evaluate final reports from review teams and agree a course of action.
5) Make recommendations on policy matters to policy committee (eg redeployment or redundancy policies).

Above all, the committee would follow up recommendations against agreed timetables to ensure that the necessary action had been taken.

The composition and powers of the controlling committee will of course vary depending on whether it is in central or local government or in a public utility, and will be particularly influenced by the respective powers of elected representatives, lay members and officers. However, the principles of control will not alter greatly between say central and local government. Indeed, the suggested composition and duties of the local government performance review committees described here are not dissimilar in concept to those of the UK Public Accounts Committee which comprises senior members of parliament.

Who undertakes the Reviews

Performance review committees and the like are of course power-less to achieve improvements to value for money without an effective and determined review team(s) to carry out the actual work. In this regard, there are a number of options open to any public sector authority in selecting the type of team best suited to the nature of the work. Broadly, the choice lies between one or a combination of the following:

1) A part-time team of elected members and/or officers.
2) A team of officers selected from within the department to be reviewed.
3) A team of officers drawn from other departments.
4) A team from management services, internal audit or other central department.
5) External management consultants.

If any impact is to be made by the VFM reviews then it may be necessary to invest many man-months of intensive work in a project. For example, Price Waterhouse recently reviewed the purchasing and stores arrangements for a large Metropolitan Authority which took about 75 man-weeks to complete, using a team which averaged 6 people. The size and scope of most public sector reviews would seem to rule out the use of a part-time team.

It is also unlikely that a team of officers selected entirely from within a department would have the objectivity with which to recommend perhaps unpopular measures affecting the careers and responsibilities of close colleagues. On the other hand it is important for people from outside the department to have an understanding of the ethos and culture of the department being reviewed. Internal Audit are ideally placed to provide assistance on VFM reviews but unfortunately the standard of internal audit in the public sector has not been generally very good. It has been seen as a 'necessary evil' for ensuring that the conduct of those responsible for operating an organisation remains within prescribed rules, regulations and legislation. Value for money auditing has remained at a fairly low level in most public sector authorities although this is noticeably not the case in such organisations as the General Accounting Office in the USA and the Auditor General's department in Canada.

Ideally, therefore, the team should comprise a full-time multidisciplinary unit of mature and experienced people. It should provide a blend of staff who understand the workings and background of the department under review combined with the objectivity of reasonably senior people outside it. Where possible suitably qualified professional reviewers from a central management services unit should be included in the team. Alternatively use may be made of outside consultants who, providing they are properly briefed and directed, can make a significant contribution through their independent approach and knowledge of other organisations both in the public and private sectors.

If consultants are used it is of course essential that they work closely with departmental management, but it should be made clear at the outset, that the final recommendations should be those of the consultants. In other words while the officers in a department will be invaluable in explaining the rationale behind the department's decisions, in obtaining the data for the review more quickly than would be possible by the consultants and in discussing the practicability of the consultants' ideas, they should not be asked to present the recommendations themselves. Firstly, this approach might jeopardise the objectivity of the findings and secondly if the consultants take responsibility for the recommendations then the departmental officer can continue to work with his colleagues without strain or embarrassment.

APPENDIX 1 A CHECKLIST FOR REVIEWING SPENDING*

1. *Employees Expenses*

Role of the Trade Unions;
Agency Services;
Staffing Flexibility;
Directly Employed Staff and Contract Employment;
   Operating Expenditure;
   Capital Programmes;
Labour Intensive and Plant Intensive Working;
Overtime Working;
Rationalisation of Staffing Structures;
Training;
Administration;
Budgeting for Employees Expenses.

2. *Premises Expenses*

Large Element of Fixed Costs;
Rationalising the Use of Premises;
Repair and Maintenance;
   Responsibility and Practice;
   Planned Maintenance;
Maintenance of Grounds;
Fuel, Light, Cleaning Materials and Water;
   Tariffs;
   Plant Efficiency
   Insulation;
   Water;
   Heating and Ventilation;
   Hours and Periods of Use;
   Furniture and Fittings;
   Rent and Rates;
   Design of Buildings.

3. *Supplies and Services*

Central Supply Organisation;
Using Supplies and Services;
   Equipment;

* *Source*: ''Cost Reduction in Public Authorities — A View'', CIPFA, 1979

Provisions;
Other Supplies;
Contracted Services;
Contracts;
Procedure;
Frequency;
Form;
Catchment Area;
Evaluation;
Stocks and Inventories;
Stores Organisation;
Stores Records;
Inventories;
Computer Methods;
Financing;
Methods;
Operating Consequence;
Budgetary Practices.

4. *Transport and Plant Expenses*

Co-ordinated Transport Management;
Operation and Deployment;
Fleet Capacity and Demand;
Specialist Vehicles and Plant;
Multi-Purpose Vehicles and Plant Pooling;
Suitability for Main Purpose;
Staffing;
Fuel Facilities;
Licensing;
Costing and Records;
Maintenance and Servicing;
Siting of Depots;
Spares;
Tyres;
Servicing Schedules;
Replacements and Additions;
Allowances to Staff.

5. *Establishment Expenses*

Printing Arrangements;
Stationery;
Advertising;
Postages;

Telephones;
Travelling, Conference and Subsistence Expenses;
Insurance.

6. *Agency Services*

Inter-Departmental Agencies;
Inter-Authority Agencies;
Joint Operations by Public Authorities;
Voluntary Organisations.

7. *Miscellaneous Expenses*

Subscriptions;
Grants to Voluntary Associations;
Other Expenses.

8. *Debt Charges*

Cash Flow Management;
Non-Borrowing Sources of Finance;
   Government Capital Grants;
   Contribution from Revenue;
   Internal Capital Funding;
   Leaseback, Leasing and Renting;
   Capital Receipts;
Borrowing Techniques;
Overall Considerations.

9. *Income*

Excludes Central and Local Taxation;
Government Grants;
Sales;
   Publications;
   Produce;
   Catering;
   Miscellaneous Sales;
Fees and charges;
Rents;
Housing;
Commercial and Industrial Rents;
Operational Rents;
Miscellaneous Rents;

Interest Receivable;
Other Sources of Income, eg Lotteries, Advertising
Sales.

10. Capital Expenditure

Long-Term Nature of Capital Investments;
Capital Plans;
Capital Programmes;
Capital Projects;
  Strict Budgetary Controls;
  Performance and Monitoring.

APPENDIX 2   UNION CONSULTATIVE ARRANGEMENTS FOR A VFM
REVIEW*

Introduction

1 In our experience it is essential that there are defined and recognised
   procedures for consultation with members, officers and trade union
   representatives during the review. Set out below are details of the
   normal consultative arrangements which would be followed in the
   case of an assignment.

Departmental level

2 On receiving instructions to commence the assignment a departmental 'set up' meeting would be arranged which would be attended
   by the following:

(1) Chairman of the committee.
(2) Director and appropriate senior managers.
(3) Departmental trade union representatives and appropriate branch
    officials.
(4) Audit staff.

3 The purpose of this meeting is:

(1) To introduce the audit staff.
(2) To discuss in broad terms the scope of the review, the way that the
    audit staff will approach it and the timetable to be followed.

* *Source*: Price Waterhouse/Gee and Company, Value for Money Auditing Manual.

(3) To agree the arrangements for consultation including:
    a) frequency and format of ongoing progress meetings and who will attend from elected members, management, trades unions and the auditors
    b) arrangements for introducing the audit staff to employees with whom they will come into contact during the review
    c) consultation on draft reports.

4 Once the review is underway there would be regular progress meetings so that the audit staff can report on progress to date, on the future programme and discuss any queries or problems.

5 Before the final report or summary is presented to the committee, meetings would be arranged with members, officers and trade union representatives to discuss the auditor's findings and recommendations.

Conclusion

6 The consultation process is a constructive aid to the successful performance of an assignment and we would comply with any consultative arrangements which are agreed by the authority. The time spent in consultation should, however, be properly recognised bearing in mind the tight reporting deadlines which are a part of most assignments.

7 Combating Waste

*'Yet another pressure to spend comes from the need to
uphold prestige. This argument was used endlessly to
justify lavish accommodation, luxurious furniture, bigger
cars, better kept lawns and flower beds and even high staff
gradings and salaries.'*

Leslie Chapman

The media have somehow fostered the idea in the minds of the
public that waste is a feature of all levels of government both local
and central.

Hardly a day goes by without a new horror story about extravagance in the public service being printed in the popular press.
These stories easily gain root in the imagination of the man in the
street, firstly because he often takes a perverse pleasure in
believing that his hard-earned cash is being frittered away by
faceless bureaucrats, but more seriously because he has no yardsticks for measuring whether he is getting value for money or not.
Although legislation, such as the UK Planning and Land Act
1980, has caused there to be much more accountability in local
government undertakings, for example, in the form of productivity and output indicators in published accounts, generally
the public has no means of evaluating whether service outputs
justify the money spent on producing them.

From our experience waste is far from being a feature of the
public sector, indeed, the majority of officials in it are hard-
working and able people who are as cost conscious as their
counterparts in any other large undertaking. There is certainly
plenty of evidence of waste in large private sector organisations.
Unfortunately, a number of factors conspire to prevent the public
sector official from being motivated to initiate rigorous cost
reduction programmes. Most obviously there is an absence of the
profit incentive. Secondly, there is the problem inherent in most
types of public undertaking, but particularly in central government departments, that officials are not clearly accountable for

the resources they consume. All too often common costs such as stationery, heating and lighting and depreciation are accounted for centrally and not by the people using them. Thirdly, the present system of annualised cash budgets, whereby if you do not spend money by the end of the year you forgo it, does not exactly encourage thrift. Last, and perhaps most importantly, officials in the public sector gain no reward for economising. Indeed, the local government leisure services director (a favourite target for cuts) for example will often have the doubtful pleasure of seeing hard-won savings being handed over to another department (often Education or Social Services) to spend.

Unlike the private sector, the public sector does not recognise cost awareness as a desirable management virtue to be rewarded by cash or promotion. All too frequently the most important item on the appraisal form is 'ability to get on with colleagues and subordinates'. An admirable trait no doubt but not one designed to lead to significant savings, especially having regard to the fact that up to 75% of all savings are likely to stem from staff costs.

Having regard to all of these factors it is perhaps surprising that waste is not more widespread. Nonetheless, it is true that there are considerable opportunities for savings in even the best run organisation as we indicated earlier. In referring to these opportunities it should be stressed that we are not talking about the waste arising from well intentioned but ultimately disastrous policy decisions. These, although relating to vast sums of money as in the case of the De Lorean débâcle, are beyond the scope of this book.

We are writing about waste and extravagance in the more orthodox sense; waste involved in paying too much for supplies, in maintaining unnecessarily high levels of stock and in paying two men to do a job which could be comfortably handled by one. We are therefore talking about everyday examples of waste which are often under our noses. The type of saving highlighted in Mr Leslie Chapman's book 'Your Disobedient Servant' in which a suggestion from a chargehand/electrician at a RAF base saved £40,000 per year. His revolutionary suggestion was to turn off gas cookers in the mess kitchens when not in use. Scores of examples such as this could be given but that would be to trivialise the subject. Nevertheless, the example shows that one does not need to go far afield to make savings, which although perhaps small in themselves, cumulatively become material. Our experience (as consultants) indicates that, on average, savings of 10% can be expected from an independent cost review. Sir Derek Rayner, in responding to questions from a select committee on his efficiency reviews in the British Civil Service stated that: 'In areas where staffing was the issue between 11% to 45% could be saved'.

The now celebrated Leslie Chapman cost reviews in the Southern Region of the Ministry of Public Buildings and Works found that, 'on the basis of two experimental reports, savings of anything up to 30% of the total expenditure could be won and this is what we achieved'.

The savings then, are there to be discovered. We have found from the wide range of value for money studies carried out by Price Waterhouse that a number of common areas emerge as offering opportunities for saving regardless of the type of authority. These areas are discussed later. However, it should be stressed that far reaching as many of these cost reduction initiatives may be, it is always necessary to look behind them to see whether an even more fundamental questioning should be made. While therefore it is valid to ask of every activity 'can it be carried out more economically?' or 'can a better service be provided at no extra cost?', managers should be also asking 'should this activity be carried out at all?' Has the reason for the activity long since disappeared? For example, there is no point in introducing sophisticated fuel conservation measures in buildings which are hardly occupied, yet this has happened for example in the case of cavernous mental hospitals built in Victorian times where occupancy has been dramatically reduced through community care measures. The example also comes to mind of the local authority who continued to budget for smoke control grant application officers when smoke control grants had been withdrawn for that particular authority.

Some of the examples quoted below may appear somewhat obvious. So obvious in fact that it might appear odd that it has taken so long for many public sector organisations to take action in the areas so highlighted. This can often be put down to civil service inertia or what has been called 'entrenched lethargy', partly for the reasons mentioned earlier but also because carefully constructed empires are not lightly relinquished. Often elaborate reasons are given for resisting change but perhaps the most common is that the authority or department 'does not have the resources to carry out the review or the changes required'.

Yet very often enormous potential savings are lost year after year for the lack of investment in an investigation team, perhaps a handful of people. The public sector is generally not very good at investing money to gain long term savings because a week in politics is indeed a long time. Nevertheless, it is ironic that as consultants we find when we come to discuss wasteful practices which perhaps have been going on for decades, that the department by coincidence already has in hand the improvements we suggest. This perhaps proves there is invariably slack in any organisation which if taken up can provide the necessary resources. For example, Chapman says it would be interesting to find out how many people in central government departments have been refused leave because of pressure of work. By inference these would be very few. He points out that in the British Civil Service, leave may only be granted if the work situation permits. Taking a staff of say 1,000 entitled to say 5 weeks each there will always be about 100 staff on leave – enough for many value for money teams. He also said that a report in the *Daily Telegraph* about a check on telephone calls in 1976 showed that some 5,000 calls had been made over 3 or 4 days in a particular department to obtain cricket scores. These anecdotes serve to show that time can always be found to save money if management is determined enough.

In considering common areas for savings we have concentrated upon the two major areas which are likely to provide the most opportunities for saving, namely manpower and the procurement of supplies and services. However, many other areas such as maintenance costs often provide savings and we have also touched briefly on these areas. We have not dealt directly with opportunities for savings arising from the 'contracting out' of services to the private sector because we consider this topic justifies a chapter of its own.

MANPOWER COSTS

Manpower costs account for the bulk of public sector expenses and therefore any serious cost reduction programme will be forced to address this sensitive area. Considerable political will is necessary to break down entrenched establishments and to clear away restrictive practices. Unpopular decisions have to be made. However, as mentioned earlier, it is our experience that when staff reductions do become necessary the effects can be minimised by a sympathetic approach and careful planning and the worst fears of management, staff and unions alleviated.

A combination of genuine redeployment, early retirement and natural turnover can normally avoid the problems of involuntary redundancies. There is no doubt that the economic recession has brought with it a new air of reality amongst trade union members. This awareness by trade unions manifests itself in many ways, for example many refuse collection work forces have voluntarily shed a large percentage of their number to beat private tenders. One reads of the recent case of construction workers in Newark, New Jersey striking because they felt that the wage increase they had been awarded was too high and detrimental to their long term interests. However, Unions fear the arbitrary 'across the board' percentage cuts which may be forced on an organisation through lack of proper manpower planning and it is this situation which inevitably leads to friction. They will respond more favourably to redundancies where manning levels have been reviewed in a scientific way and where staff reductions are handled in an orderly and phased manner.

Top Heavy Organisations

Staffing levels and structures in organisations have often evolved from situations which occurred many years ago and which have not since been reviewed. For example the 1974 local government re-organisation in the UK, whereby many authorities were merged or taken over, appears in retrospect to have resulted in organisational structures designed more to protect existing staff than to fit the operational needs of the new authorities.

It is therefore appropriate to examine the rationale behind public sector structures. We have found as a general rule that public sector departments are top heavy and often have 'one-over-one' organisational relationships which not only create an unnecessary level of management but also slow down decision making. Where therefore the classic pyramid shaped structure is usually found in commercial organisations the equivalent in the public sector tends to be 'pear shaped'. For example, during the 1974 re-organisation a large number of 'deputy' departmental director posts were created which had no line responsibilities of their own and merely tended to mirror the activities of the directors, eg both attending the same committee meetings.

We had occasion recently to review a leisure and recreation services department for a large metropolitan borough, which provided an example of what Chapman calls 'pyramidosis', namely swollen staff complements accompanied by an excess of supervision. In this example, the management structure was as follows:

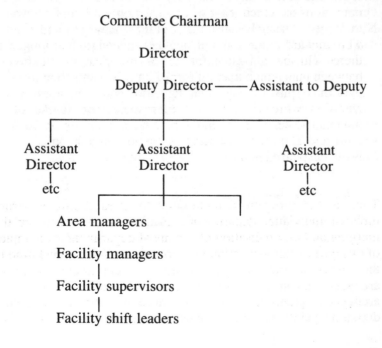

In this case therefore, between the humble user of the swimming pool or sports centre, and the committee chairman there were seven levels of supervision. It is suggested that had a commercial leisure undertaking had to support the crushing weight of this organisation it would have been out of business very quickly. One of the main defences of this structure was that a high level of supervision was necessary to the safety of the users, especially young bathers. However, professional people, and this includes not only leisure specialists, but all professionally qualified people such as engineers, accountants and architects should only need a minimum of supervision. Unfortunately, the public sector often feels obliged to introduce totally unnecessary levels of supervision. Not only therefore do these people waste their own time and that of their subordinates but often they are obliged to report on their activities which of course requires the full panoply of clerks, typists, messengers and drivers.

As Leslie Chapman so aptly puts it:

> If for example 50 processors are part of a unit performing operations to which the processors contribute only a part, the unit will have its own management structure and may well include other functional pyramids. Either way then there will be almost limitless possibilities for clashes between management and the upper levels of the functional pyramids pushing to defend their special interests. Decisions which should take minutes drag on for weeks and months, while costs, in staff time and administration, soar upwards. The use of the accountable management structure is the best cure for this problem provided the managers are given powers to lop off the tops of the pyramids.

There is therefore considerable scope for streamlining the structures of individual departments. Further scope exists for the merging and rationalisation of groups of departments. Examples of this type of rationalisation in local government can be found in the dispersal of the functions of a planning department to finance, architects, housing and engineering or in the merging of the architects, planning, engineers and environmental health departments into a single technical services department. In either example, fewer senior officers may be required. In this regard, Figure 7.1 illustrates the ratios of staff to management for a variety of services in a large Metropolitan Borough, while the levels of responsibility are not directly comparable between departments the range of differences is interesting.

FIGURE 7.1   *Ratio of Staffing Levels/Senior Management by Department*

Department	Number of senior officers*	Number of monthly paid staff	Average number of staff controlled
Social Services	3	399	133
Planning	4	98	25
Housing	5	268	54
Architectural Services	3	94	31
Engineering Services	2	171	85
Legal and Administration	4	139	35
Leisure and Recreation	3	259	86
Education	5	179	36
Environmental Health	4	93	23
Finance	5	270	54

*Assistant directors, deputy and director

Activity Levels

There is often a tendency in the public sector for staffing levels not to respond as quickly as they should to either declining activity levels, especially it seems in respect of the administrative 'tail', or changes in legislation which effectively take away functions. At central government level in the UK the number of civil servants rose from 660,000 to 750,000 over the period 1966 to 1976, an outstanding rate of growth. Undoubtedly, a range of new services has had to be absorbed requiring more people. Equally, there has been a reduction in many services but these have not always led to lower staffing levels.

An example of this at local government level occurred during a review of an architect's department employing about 150 architects, quantity surveyors and other technicians who handled annually about £25 million of building contracts. Early on in the review it became apparent that had all the design and quantity surveying work of the department been placed with outside professional firms the total notional fees would have been much less than the running costs of the department. This finding suggested that the department was overstaffed and this was borne out when the individual work loads of the staff were studied. In particular, it was found that while the total value of contracts on hand had dropped from £32 million in 1976 to £25 million in 1979, the number of senior architects for example had increased (despite the work mix remaining the same) from 18 to 24.

A similar situation was found with quantity surveyors, clerks of works and administrative staff. In addition, the projected work loads showed further decline over the next five years. Yet had an outside objective review not been carried out it is unlikely that attention would have been drawn to the overmanning. In total it was possible to reduce staff levels by about half, in line with the reduction in capital works which had also halved over the period. Despite the large reductions which were made it was possible to achieve them gradually with no enforced redundancy.

The resultant slimmed-down department was not only much more economical and efficient but the morale was far higher. Despite some views to the contrary local government officers are normally conscientious people who are not happy when underemployed. The measure of this unhappiness is borne out by the fact that when interviewed the members of the architect's department freely admitted to their lack of work and many interesting tales were told of cottages being renovated or small businesses being run in office hours!

This example led to savings in the region of £½ million per year, a relatively small sum in itself but how many times could the saving be repeated in other local government authorities. The message to be gained from the exercise is that if a simple set of key performance measures are used to monitor the productivity of a department then imbalances in the staff/activity ratio will soon be spotted. In this case a yardstick was established for both architects and quantity surveyors relating to average contract values and this was used after the review to monitor the ongoing productivity of the department.

Apart from the need to keep an eye on activity levels it is also necessary to monitor the effects of changes in working methods and legislation in terms of possible staff savings. While the costs and savings of large scale projects such as the introduction of computers and word processing installations will normally be carefully evaluated, often less publicised events will go unnoticed. This state of affairs may be called the 'gas fitter' syndrome. It is said that a Northern authority employed four gas fitters solely to attend to the council's street gaslamps. Unfortunately for the fitters it was realised eventually that the council had changed completely to electric light some years before and that therefore their services would have to be redeployed. The irony of the situation is that the council only discovered this small enclave of gas fitters when, through their union spokesman, they demanded that the size of their unit justified the establishment of a foreman.

Though the story may be slightly apocryphal the message is clear. All too often labour saving methods are introduced but the establishment remains the same. This is particularly true in maintenance sections where the largest allocation of time on the worker's timesheet is often to 'general duties', or 'routine maintenance work'. In reviews we have carried out on maintenance departments the allocation to these headings has been as high as 40% where maintenance staff were not carrying out specific duties but merely filling in time. Perhaps these examples are indications that management in the public sector, because of a lack of accountability, are more easily able to maintain the status quo and to keep their empires intact than is the case in the private sector. Certainly, this environment provides a useful umbrella for maintaining numerous restrictive practices. These can range from large scale examples in central government or public utilities to smaller but very numerous examples in local government. As an example of the former we can point to British Rail who had, under trade union pressure, for a long time after the full conversion to diesel and electric trains retained a second man on the footplate, who had been the fireman in the days of steam. As an example of the latter we noted the practice of a local authority of sending out two mechanics to help drivers change tyres on their vehicles. The unfortunate private sector driver changes his own tyres.

Square Pegs

A further phenomenon in the public sector is that many authorities make a virtue out of employing the right person in the wrong job and vice versa. For example, it is not uncommon for local government officers to become promoted but to retain almost an identical job specification. For instance we came across a competent and intelligent assistant director of an environmental health department who spent a great deal of time carrying out laboratory tests which a laboratory assistant could have carried out for a third of the salary. In another instance we noted a senior finance officer whose salary was in the region of £12,000 per year employed for most of his time in delivering the department's internal mail. One could not envisage a cost conscious finance director in the private sector allowing that situation to continue.

Conversely the public sector are often reluctant to employ the specialist expertise which is necessary for a particular post; for example, it is well known that the British Treasury has few qualified accountants relative to its size. This 'generalist' approach, whereby an intelligent civil servant is supposed to take in his stride an overnight change from say customs and excise to computer auditing, not only discourages a high level of professional management but can also be expensive.

This situation has been recognised in the UK police service where a number of investigations are being carried out to pursue opportunities for 'civilianisation', ie to increase the use of civilians to take over posts previously held by policemen or women. The initiative for these reviews has come from the UK Audit Commission in consultation with the Home Office and others with the object of improving productivity and/or reducing costs to ratepayers. The Audit Commission has estimated that it costs roughly £6,000 less to employ a civilian than it does to employ a uniformed person to do the same job after taking into account shift payments and other prerequisites. More important perhaps than the cost element however, is the fact that civilians can release uniformed men from routine jobs such as process servers, telephonists and driving instructors to 'front line duties'.

Administrative Posts

As indicated earlier the 'administrative tail' often remains intact even though retrenchment has taken place in respect of staff actually providing services to the public. It is curious that although work study methods and productivity schemes have been with us on the 'shop floor' since the 'thirties' very few inroads have been made into the clerical or administrative area. Yet when studies of productivity have been carried out very wide differences in work rate have been observed between departments, divisions, sections and individuals, even in cases where there was no discernible difference between them in working conditions or methods.

As an example, we carried out a review of the productivity of library assistants over some 20 branch libraries. It was found that the rate of issues varied from 28 to 49 per hour. On the basis of the findings a comfortable target rate was introduced of about 40 issues per hour which led to significant staff savings.

In a major review of the clerical functions of a water authority wide differences were discovered in the output achieved by various divisions for such systems as payroll, debtors and creditor payment. For example, the number of sundry debtor invoices raised per clerk varied by as much as from 1 to 4 per hour. However, when further comparisons were made with the outside world using such units as engineering companies and other public utilities, the output of even the more productive divisions was only a third of private sector organisations. Indeed, the water authority was spending almost eight times as much on accounting and administration as a private sector manufacturing company of equivalent turnover.

While the examples given are fairly low level they are indicative of the poor clerical productivity in many public undertakings; furthermore, when the possible savings are added together they reach major proportions. In the case of the water authority, savings of over £1 million per annum were achieved through rationalisation and increased productivity in the clerical and financial procedures. Indeed it has been calculated that if only one clerk per local authority in England and Wales was saved it would be equivalent to about £3 million per year.

Overtime and Bonus Payments

Overtime and bonus payments often provide a fruitful source of saving and both should be carefully monitored. A review of overtime working can be revealing in terms of its extent, nature and reasons and in balancing costs with the alternatives available. As overtime involves enhanced rates of pay, and often other additional overhead costs, it may be possible for alternatives, such as increasing the normal establishment, to produce savings. Persistent and excessive overtime is often a symptom of inefficient working methods or practices. It also raises the question as to whether or not productivity during normal working hours is as high as it should be.

It is an accepted fact that staff regularly working long hours become jaded and the law of diminishing returns sets in. This is perhaps particularly true of clerical functions where the mental processes only remain sharp for relatively short concentrated periods. In situations were consistently high levels of overtime are being worked on clerical tasks, a simple logging system should be introduced to record the numbers of transactions (eg invoices raised per day) processed and suitable comparative checks made on productivity levels with other offices, departments or organisations as appropriate.

Bonus payments can also provide significant savings. In many local government authorities bonus schemes are regularly paying maximum bonuses. In the circumstances therefore, the incentive element is lost.

In addition these inefficient schemes will often cost a great deal to administer. In some instances, it is possible to tighten up individual schemes whilst in others the opportunity may exist to either consolidate bonus payments into the weekly wage or to 'buy out' the bonus element. From our experience this approach has led to considerable savings in the number of work study officers and bonus clerks attached to the bonus scheme in a wide diversity of areas such as vehicle maintenance, housing maintenance, refuse collection, parks maintenance and sewer cleansing. After all it is totally nonsensical to pay this type of staff to administer a scheme which never fails to pay the maximum allowed. However, once the bonus element is dropped from the remuneration package then it becomes more important for an adequate level of supervision to be maintained to ensure that a fair days work is done for a fair days pay.

PURCHASING OF SUPPLIES AND SERVICES

The public sector is a very substantial buyer of goods and services. For example, annual purchases for local government alone in England and Wales amount to over £2 billion per year. The scale of spending in itself in this area demands attention. However, it is an area where an accumulation of relatively small savings on specific items, rather than large dramatic discoveries, makes the main impact. In other words major savings are to be had but only through painstaking attention to detail and the determination to ensure the most economic purchases are made for every item. In short, public sector employees have to be motivated to act as though they are spending their own money. Furthermore, the achievement of large savings requires close liaison between different functions and departments in an authority and indeed between authorities. This liaison is often lacking.

The Audit Commission for Local Authorities in England and Wales, has stated that improved purchasing arrangements can lead to savings of the order of 5−8%. A saving of say 5% in even a small district council could release funds of around £40,000 to £50,000 a year for more useful purposes. In the case of a large Metropolitan Council or government department, the savings could amount to several millions. This should come as no surprise since many studies in the private and public sectors have confirmed that more aggressive and skillful buying can reduce costs substantially. The Audit Commission itself recently carried out a special study into purchasing in conjunction with the auditors of local authorities. Part of the study entailed comparing the purchase costs of all authorities for a 'basket' of 45 common items, as diverse as video cassettes, paving slabs and refuse sacks. The study highlighted among other things the enormous variation in the prices paid for even prosaic items despite making allowances for economies of scale and geographical factors.

The scope of the Audit Commission study was wide ranging and identified four main initiatives that have been helpful to authorities in reducing the detailed costs of bought-in goods and services. The initiatives echo our experience in reducing purchasing costs and are worth examining in detail:

1) Changing the specification of the items purchased to eliminate excessive variety or to reduce unnecessarily high standards of design or material.
2) 'Shopping around' more aggressively for supplies.
3) Taking full advantage of purchasing scale.
4) Managing storage and distribution facilities more efficiently.

Changing Specifications

Due to the often wide range of users of common items in the public sector, opportunities exist for rationalising specifications and where possible specifying items that suppliers can manufacture more cheaply. Often items such as stationery, microcomputers and even vehicles represent every whim and fancy of the recipients. For example, we found in one large Metropolitan Borough with a reputation for tight management, that their education department was regularly purchasing more than 150 different types of exercise books. The number was subsequently reduced to 7 with the active involvement and support of teachers and with major cost savings resulting.

Scope often exists for changing quality specifications where the risks involved are judged acceptable. The value analysis technique whereby the quality and volume of every purchase item are examined critically, is an approach which has been used with considerable success in the private sector. It has not been accepted so successfully in the public sector and often quality specifications are too high. The value analysis process should be applied to all areas from the size of cars hired for the use of civil servants to more mundane items such as the quality of paper used in printing or photocopying equipment.

Obtaining Competitive Quotations

Most government departments have strict rules related to tendering procedures for obtaining goods and services. While these procedures are often the most effective in ensuring that undue bias is not shown to particular suppliers and to minimise the opportunities for fraud they do not always act as effectively in ensuring that the most competitive quotations are received. For example, we have found that with one large education authority substantial tenders were invited whch made allowance only for quoting list prices. No information was given as to the possible value or quantities of supplies required. This situation meant that new suppliers had no information on which to base their prices, and even existing suppliers would only be aware of past supplies to the department, and not the whole picture. Substantial discounts were thus lost. During the same study we found a number of other anomalies in the tendering process for educational supplies, in particular:

1) There was no request for details as to how long the prices would be fixed.
2) Only the four main suppliers were listed for the purchasing committee's approval even though tenders had been obtained from a number of other suppliers. The suppliers not included on the list offered lower prices for 21% of the items.
3) The documents provided by Central Purchasing were not used in their entirety. Certain contractual clauses were omitted from the final document produced by the Educational Supplies

FIGURE 7.2   *Plant Hire Costs*

Item	Council's Supplier	Another Local Authority Supplier
Kango 900 Hammer		
per day	£10.00	£ 7.50
each additional day	£ 3.60	£ 1.50
7 days	£32.40	£12.50
36ft extension ladder	£ 9.90	£ 8.00

Source: Audit Commission for Local Government in England and Wales.

Section. As an example, a clause was included referring to special conditions but no special conditions were sent with the tender document.

Officers responsible for purchasing should always be vigilant for opportunities for keener prices. Analyses of the prices paid for similar commodities (often from the same suppliers) by different local government authorities have frequently disclosed major opportunities for saving. For example, Figure 7.2 opposite shows a typical comparison of the cost of hiring small plant. The council concerned is an outer London Borough with a good reputation for tight management. In the education department review mentioned earlier, we noted many similar examples of best available prices not being obtained, eg:

1) Sellotape and similar lines purchased from the main stationery supplier cost up to twice as much as from any other supplier.
2) The majority of office equipment purchases and stationery obtained from three main suppliers could have been obtained at anything between 18% and 40% cheaper at another supplier.

Overall, the analysis of selected lines showed that savings of 12% on the total expenditure involved (about £450,000) could be made if best prices had been obtained at each opportunity.

The above is a small example, but multiplied by the many thousands of items purchased in the public sector accumulatively adds up to a great deal of money. A further weak area in obtaining competitive quotations is that invoice prices are often not checked back against agreed tender prices. In a review which we carried out for a large Metropolitan Borough Council we found the authority had been charged more than the agreed price for items in over 20% of the cases. The Audit Commission also gives the example of an authority where a long-standing supplier increased invoice prices by 14.5% when the agreed figure was 6.5%. This was scarcely surprising since the department receiving the goods had no information on the agreed price.

Taking Advantage of Scale

As we implied earlier individual public sector authorities are large organisations with often a very large number of ordering points for common items. Because of this there are often considerable opportunities to negotiate discounts in return for extra guaranteed volume to the supplier. In particular there are many instances where different departments within a local government authority (or indeed different units within a single service such as education) are buying common items at different prices, often from the same supplier. Subject to constraints such as quality specifications there is often much to be said for arranging central negotiation to ensure that the full advantages of scale are realised.

The examination of a large health region revealed that many identical items were ordered independently by districts within the region. The items ranged from ambulances to micro-computers, typing paper and bandages. Had the full economies of scale been taken, opportunities for saving around £5 million per annum could have been exploited. In a local government county authority an analysis showed that over 30 establishments were making their own arrangements for the purchase of meat and groceries despite the existence of apparently more favourable contracts negotiated by the county. Many of the officers in charge were unaware (or claimed to be) of the county contracts.

FIGURE 7.3 *Difference from Nominated Supplier Price (%)*	
L/H Drainer sink	plus 130%
Hacksaw blades	88%
Typist chair	76%
Hardboard	40%
Paving mortar	11%
Source: Audit Commission	

Similarly, there are many cases where individual purchasing officers have failed to take advantage of centrally negotiated prices. Figure 7.3 opposite shows the results of an Audit Commission survey into purchasing for an outer London Borough where differences between the price actually paid by the Council for the most recent purchase of a particular item and the delivered price of the nominated supplier were widespread.

We came across a further example in a purchasing review of colleges of further education. The comparison of costs for maintenance of units between the supplier used by the college and the supplier used by the parent local authority was as shown in Figure 7.4.

FIGURE 7.4

Central Contact price	*College prices*
(for 3 visits per year)	(for 2 visits per year)
Electric machine £11 per machine	£20 per machine
Manual machine £5 per machine	£9.60 per machine

Experience also shows that considerable opportunities exist for taking advantage of consortia either for individual items or for a collection of purchase items. While there is often good reason for an authority to purchase on its own account, nonetheless consortium arrangements can often provide the opportunity to obtain lower prices. Figure 7.5 below shows a further analysis prepared by the Audit Commission which illustrates the differences between the prices routinely paid by a London Borough and the Greater London Council price for the same item.

FIGURE 7.5 *London Borough Prices Paid % Excess over GLC Price*

Typist's chair	106%
Paper towels	62%
Microphone	50%
Industrial gloves	31%

Source: Audit Commission

Storage and Distribution

Purchasing is concerned with the total delivered cost and not just with aggressively negotiated purchase prices. Management will want to be satisfied that where goods are taken into and delivered from central stores, as opposed to delivered directly by the supplier to the ultimate consumer, the total cost of storage and distribution is more than covered by the lower price achieved. This calculation must take into account all the costs for storage including administrative and overhead costs and distribution costs including all transport costs such as depreciation and maintenance of vehicles. In many cases it may be found that some of the slower moving items are better called off on demand from the supplier who in effect would be carrying the storage costs. This is particularly the case with building stores where the storekeeper often knows well in advance when particular items will be required.

Leslie Chapman refers to the Portland Naval base stores where a survey revealed the prohibitively high cost of maintaining stores compared with the value of the goods being issued. It was calculated that it cost over £3 to issue even the simplest piece of equipment such as a tap washer. The review proved conclusively that small items could be bought locally, more quickly and easily as and when they were wanted and that larger items could be stored centrally and issued when required. The review concluded that it would be possible to close three stores depots completely through this rationalisation after allowing for the extra costs involved in transport from central stores, and the savings were of the order of 80 − 90% of the earlier storage and distribution costs.

A feature of stores in the public sector is that excessively high service standards are often the norm. It is important that stock re-order levels reflect current usage rather than inspired guess-work. In many cases stock levels are held at the discretion of the storekeeper who is often a relatively junior member of the hierarchy. His actions are often dictated by his not wishing ever to be caught out by not having stock available when required. Consequently mountainous levels of stocks are held with no regard to what the economic level should be, how critical the user department would regard 'stock outs' of particular lines and how easily an item may be purchased locally if a stock out occurs.

This book is not the place to discuss scientific re-ordering levels, there are many excellent works on the subject. However, it is clear that there is considerable scope in the public sector for the introduction of more scientific stock control systems where demand is related to re-order levels and purchasing lead times. Indeed having regard to the fact that housing, water, plant and vehicle maintenance depots for instance may need to carry several thousand lines it is unlikely that this task could be accomplished without the use of computer equipment. We have come across many examples where manual stores systems have produced strange stock imbalances because they had not responded quickly enough to changes in patterns of demand. In one recent case it was reported that in the last 12 months of the life of a six-wheeled refuse vehicle, sixteen remoulded tyres were purchased; and in the same authority a total of fifty new tyres were ordered for five (four-wheeled) vehicles in 15 months.

At a large Metropolitan Borough enough stocks of brass tap fittings for 2,000 weeks of supply were found together with seven years' supply of a brand of industrial soap. Both items could have been purchased 'off the shelf' at nearby stockists.

From our experience of reviewing public sector stores organisations we have concluded that on average there is scope for reducing stock levels by at least 20% with a consequent release of a considerable amount of working capital. In one recent examination of a large city council, the introduction of a more scientific reordering system linked to on-line enquiry stations at stores sub-depots, which enabled the availability of items and other depots to be checked quickly, led to a one-off reduction of around £250,000 with an ongoing saving of interest charges.

Energy Costs

Energy costs represent such a significant proportion of an authority's purchase budget, particularly in the heating and lighting of its premises, that this item of expenditure is worth separate comment. Again it is not within the scope of this book to provide a manual on energy conservation. This has been dealt with in much more depth in many other publications. However, it is perhaps worth highlighting the main areas of potential saving.

Our experience of energy conservation reviews has been that considerable savings can result merely by introducing good housekeeping practices even before the use of expensive monitoring equipment is considered. Energy conservation, as indeed the whole area of procurement of supplies and services, is an attractive area for review since any savings do not impinge upon service levels nor do they involve the possible disruption caused by reductions in other areas, particularly manning levels.

Often the most fruitful sources for energy conservation include:

Review of tariffs   Studies should ensure that the most favourable electricity or gas tariff for a particular building or part of a building is being used.

Review of power efficiency   The efficiency of heating equipment (eg school boilers) can be checked against the latest systems available. The critical point in cost terms for replacing equipment may well occur before it is actually replaced. Because of economic constraints there is an increasing tendency for boilers to be repaired indefinitely rather than replaced on a planned cycle. This policy may not be cost effective.

Comparison of consumption levels   Comparisons for of oil, gas, electricity and water between establishments can highlight excessive usage. Investigations may reveal a variety of reasons for these excessive consumptions including faulty equipment, such as boilers and thermostats, incorrect methods of operation, lack of interest and generally poor housekeeping and lack of motivation on the part of staff to conserve energy. Similarly a manual (or probably more practically a computerised) system can monitor the technically evaluated norms of consumption for each building against actual consumption. Variances from the norm should be investigated for their cause.

Use of monitoring and control equipment   Public sector organisations, while normally well aware of energy conservation measures, are often reluctant to spend money in order to save money. For example, the use of cost effective modern energy monitoring and thermostat control equipment in schools, colleges and other large public buildings is now well documented and a payback period of 2/3 years can be achieved.

Control of capital expenditure　Conversely, where provision for expenditure on any conservation measures does exist it may well be that this allocation is not always spent in the most cost effective way. Pressure on officers to spend this allocation may result in 'easily spent' measures being achieved, rather than those that provide the largest savings. For example there is little benefit obtained by installing an optimum start controller on an old and inefficient boiler. A review of the measures being taken should concentrate upon the forecasted payback periods, and whether these are realistic.

The use of energy conservation managers　Officers with authority-wide responsibility with perhaps a small statistical unit are now a well established concept. If energetic and experienced officers are recruited they would be expected to save their own payroll costs many times over.

OTHER AREAS OF WASTE

As we mentioned we have dwelt at some length upon the manning and purchasing areas because in most public sector authorities they are likely to provide the most opportunities for saving. However, from our experience of a wide range of value for money reviews we have found a number of other areas which almost invariably give rise to savings regardless of the type of public sector authority involved. The areas fall under the general headings of:

1) Maintenance costs
2) Land and buildings
3) Transport and plant
4) Income
5) Cash management.

Each of these areas is discussed briefly in turn.

Maintenance Costs

We have found that changes in the use of what is termed 'planned maintenance' can provide very useful economies. The problem is in balancing the risk of a breakdown (if you make the maintenance intervals too long) against spending a great deal of money unnecessarily (if you make the intervals too short). Critical items such as emergency care medical units may need to be looked at every day and yet it may still be necessary to carry out emergency repairs when required.

At the other extreme Leslie Chapman refers to a review which came across large store sheds with roofs 40 to 50 feet high where light was provided by banks of fluorescent tubes. Whenever a tube failed a couple of electricians trundled a large mobile tower to the spot and one of them climbed up and changed the tube. It took between 30 and 40 minutes to change a tube and there were so many tubes that more than one pair of electricians were kept busy. As the amount of light was not critical and it was possible to operate with up to a third of the tubes out of action the survey team concerned was able to establish an agreement for the batch replacement of all the tubes, the probable life of which could be estimated with considerable accuracy. The saving was around 80% on the original cost in this case and there were scores if not hundreds of similar cases.

The lesson to be learnt from this is that regular preventative maintenance, if it is skilfully programmed and reviewed regularly, can save a great deal of money and yet provide a service tailored to meet the needs of the users. On the other hand if it is not planned properly the potential savings are wasted. This is worth stressing because both public and private sector organisations all spend big sums annually on various forms of planned maintenance and many opportunities for economy are being overlooked. Indeed this is another area where many small items offer opportunities for savings which in themselves are not significant but which looked at accumulatively save enormous amounts of money. In general more consideration should be given to regular inspection which would permit a degree of flexibility in assessing how much and how often maintenance work should be carried out as an alternative to rigid schedules.

Many examples can be found of somewhat over zealous maintenance of premises. For example the use of modern decorating materials may allow the decoration of offices to be carried out at longer intervals. Leslie Chapman again refers to reviews of maintenance budgets in the Southern region of the Ministry of Public Buildings and Works, where savings of approximately 30% were made. The economies proposed covered almost every aspect of the organisation's activities. He points out that more grass was being cut than needed to be cut and what was needed to be cut needed less painstaking cutting. Lawn standards were pointless for grass which stretched between store sheds and was crisscrossed by overhead pipes and cables. There was no useful purpose in heating gigantic stores the size of aircraft hangers to normal office temperatures when the contents would be quite safe at lower temperatures. There was no point in maintaining a depot railway system when roads could serve just as well at a fraction of the cost. There was no need to conserve and maintain 80 or so cranes and lifting devices when experience over a long period showed that only half a dozen were needed, and that on a rare occasion when a special machine was required it could be hired at a fraction of the cost of permanent equipment.

These and many other examples indicate the scale of savings which can be made on maintenance budgets. It comes back to a critical examination of every service level as part of the overall budget or cost review process with the aim of reviewing the incremental cost of an increase or decrease. All too frequently practices such as the mowing of large areas of public open spaces which are hardly ever used are not queried even though the reason for doing them has as long since disappeared.

Land and Buildings

It is important from time to time for an objective review to be carried out of the accommodation needs of an organisation as a whole. Often the purchase of new premises can be avoided if better use is made of existing facilities. On more than one occasion we have been able to suggest the sale of cramped but prestigious high street property as a means of acquiring cheaper but roomier accommodation elsewhere. In one case a particular authority had a large building in the town centre devoted to an ill-attended museum. It was possible to arrange for the museum exhibits to be transferred to other buildings such as libraries so that the museum building could be used instead to house the overspill from the council's Leisure and Recreation Department. In yet another example we observed members of an authority's Finance Department to be 'roughing it' in temporary wooden huts while their more fortunate counterparts in the Engineering Department had the full run of a very large and roomy manor house complete wth ornamental gardens, tennis courts and other luxuries. It was possible to sell the manor house and with the proceeds to build more convenient modern offices for the department.

Even more significant savings can be achieved through the sale of surplus land. We have found with a number of local government authorities that they are not always even aware of all the land which they own.

In a review of a large Metropolitan Borough's land bank a mixed team of consultants and authority staff were set the task of searching for areas of land within the authority's boundaries which did not appear to be usefully used. Many such areas were identified, some of which were not even on the authority's land register, and although some of the areas so identified could not be sold for legal or other reasons, many others were sold for large sums of money. In particular, two or three large areas of grass land were identified which were being assiduously maintained each week and which had virtually no use as recreation areas. Furthermore these were in prime residential areas and were capable of fetching good prices. Many smaller plots were found, for example a plot was discovered by the side of one of the authority's libraries which was overgrown and neglected and which fetched £60,000 as prime residential land. The proceeds were used to provide a sorely needed extension to the library itself. Quite apart from these fairly spectacular savings however there are often a number of small plots of land adjacent to privately owned homes, the owners of which are often only too pleased to purchase when they know they are available.

The problem in many authorities is that there is often no person centrally responsible for co-ordinating and marketing surplus land in a reasonably agressive way. Often departments such as Leisure and Recreation are aware of surplus land but do not feel that it is their concern to sell it off. It is important for a senior officer to be given the task of co-ordinating the marketing of all surplus land for an authority, in liaison with professional property agents. This of course means that there needs to be reliable land registers and a formal system for the individual departments to inform the officer of surplus land as it becomes available so that it can be sold off as quickly as possible.

Transport and Plant

There are many instances of authorities using an unnecessarily wide range of vehicle types and suppliers. In these cases gradual standardisation where practical will lead to better fleet discounts and lower spares inventories being achieved.

As a general rule we have found that utilisation of vehicles tends to be on the low side in local authorities. Indeed in certain departments such as Leisure and Recreation we have found that the usage for some groups of vehicle has been as low as 17% and the mileage for a number of individual vehicles has been under 2,000 miles per year. Very often vehicle fleet sizes are geared up for peaks whereas often additional hiring, particularly for specialist vehicles, would provide a more economical approach. In a recent review for a Leisure Department it was found that over a period of six years the number of vehicles operated by the department had fallen by 6% yet the manpower of the department had fallen by 15% in the same period. This difference represented an effective growth of 24 vehicles which a more critical review of fleet replacements would have avoided.

One answer to poor utilisation is to consider more inter-departmental 'pooling' where the joint use of vehicles by, for example, the education and social services, can often be achieved.

Income

Improving an organisation's cash flow and thereby reducing debt charges is a somewhat neglected area of 'cost reduction' but can be significant and relatively painless to introduce. Potential areas of saving include the following:

Grants from Government   The availability should be reviewed to ensure that all possibilities are fully exploited. Some rather obscure grants such as those available from the European Economic Community for example can easily be overlooked.

Catering   Very many clubs and catering establishments are run by the public sector and often need to be heavily subsidised. In many instances the running of these establishments has been carried out much more efficiently by private contractors who are often willing to pay the authority a handsome fee for the privilege.

Commercial rents   Rents for commercial properties are often not very well co-ordinated in public sector organisations. This should be done on an authority-wide basis and reviewed regularly in accordance with the tenancy agreements.

Sundry debtors   Time lags between the incurring of a debt (eg the hire of a public hall, damage to public property) and the raising of the invoice is often excessive. Time lags of up to 6 months have been noted with a consequent detrimental effect on cash flow. The treasurer of a Metropolitan Borough recently mentioned that he had hired the public hall for his daughter's wedding reception and after nine months had elapsed had to remind the authority to send him a bill. Many thousands of pounds are lost in this way through poor invoicing and follow up procedures.

Charges   Charges for council facilities are often not reviewed frequently enough. We recently noted that the charge for admission for a notable and unique glass museum was only 35p. However, most of the users of the facility had travelled sometimes over 100 miles by coach to attend and therefore were not averse to paying three times the current entrance fee.

Other sources of income   An aggressive and determined survey of potential new sources of income is often worthwhile particularly in local authorities (eg lotteries, sale of produce, sale of publications, sale of old library books, advertising in rate leaflets and on refuse sacks, the lease of works of art to commercial undertakings). Where an energetic officer is given responsibility for raising additional income the results can be quite startling. For example at the London Borough of Sutton an additional £100,000 per annum in sundry income was raised for the library department through a variety of sources including using library premises on Sunday evenings for concerts, sale of prints of local scenes and the positioning of 'space invader' machines in the lobbies. The latter might not be to everybody's taste but the general approach is sound enough.

Treasury Management

A professional approach to treasury or cash flow management can often lead to extremely large savings for public sector authorities. Of particular importance is the need for a specialist officer to deal with cash flow management and a small percentage improvement in the efficient use of funds will more than repay the expense. For example, the negotiation of 2 instead of 3 days for the calculation of the period allowed for clearance of cheques with banks (value dating) can often lead to substantial savings. This is but one instance whereby faster methods for the clearance of cheques can be beneficial.

Conversely, a curious feature of some local authorities' cash management is the sometimes excessive zeal with which creditors are paid and in particular the incidence of prompt payment facilities to local creditors. One is not suggesting that creditors should be treated unfairly but often the payment terms offered by local authorities are far better than those offered by the private sector and even one day's delay in payment of creditors can have a significant effect on the interest gained. Needless to say it is necessary in these circumstances to deal with each case on its merits because a delayed payment to a small local business may cause an unbearable strain on that company's resources.

8 Budgets and Value for Money

'The annuality rule whereby if you do not spend money by the end of the financial year you forgo it. Therefore you accelerate expenditure to prevent it.'

Sir Derek Rayner

The revenue budget is normally the most detailed and authoritative financial statement that politicians receive and need to act upon, yet as a method of controlling and challenging costs and practices it has been of very limited value in most public sector organisations.

Furthermore, the preparation of the revenue budget is usually a long drawn out and often acrimonious process. Often an obsession with the minutiae of the document can result in a neglect of other, equally important management tools such as performance measurement, cost based reviews and standard costing, which are required to complement and enhance the budgeting process. The use of performance measurement in particular, adds an important dimension to the budget system we have touched on earlier.

The importance of performance measurement is that it matches input costs (eg manpower) to the quality and volume of service output (eg number of planning applications processed per month), thus allowing the productivity of an activity to be assessed; flat comparisons between budget and actual expenditure do not allow this. Also performance measurement facilitates the setting of realistic targets for budget holders, who tend to treat a budget as an easy and comfortable ally which does not require too much imagination to produce or provide much of a challenge to keep within.

In this regard, public sector budgets have all too often been based upon what was done last year plus unavoidable increases due to changes in inflation and legislation. Once approved, the budget has been considered as a 'right to spend' and there is often an unseemly scramble at the year end to make sure all the money is spent (otherwise next year's budget may be jeopardised!).

Pressures on spending at all levels of government and in most countries in the world are, as we mentioned earlier, forcing public sector organisations to question much more closely the underlying assumptions upon which budgets are based, in terms of 'do we need the activity or programme?' and if we do, 'do we need to provide such a high level of service?' These questions may to some extent be asked as a result of the 'rolling' cost based review process described earlier, although the people carrying out these reviews may not be senior enough to allow fundamental policies to be questioned. However public sector organisations are now more ready to accept the need for alternative approaches to the conventional budgetary control systems so as to provide a built-in methodology for:

1) Showing the incremental effect of introducing different levels of service.
2) Equitably ranking or prioritising apparently conflicting claims for resources.

ALTERNATIVE BUDGETING SYSTEMS

There are a wide range of alternative budgeting systems which attempt to provide suitable methodologies. Although it is not within the scope of this book to deal with them in detail, it may be helpful to touch on one or two of the better known systems in order to acquaint non-financial decision-makers with their main features. The systems we are concerned with are mostly grouped under the generic title of programme based budgeting (PBB).

Perhaps the two best known techniques in this area are Zero based budgeting (ZBB) and Programme Planning and Budgeting System (PPBS), both of which have been used for some years in the public sector, with varying degrees of success.

Zero Based Budgeting (ZBB)

This is a relatively new method of budgeting which was first used in certain States in the USA. The objective of ZBB is to design a system whereby the organisation must, for each service, programme and activity, (1) justify its existence, (2) show what level of spending is justified based on the needs of the service or programme, (3) show what level of spending is justified on the basis of past performance.

Under ZBB therefore an agency must justify its base spending and not just an incremental increase over the previous year's spending. To employ this system is thus a break with traditional budgeting methods and can involve management in considerable upheaval and discomfort during the review process.

The review process itself works from the 'bottom up', ie it begins with unit management who are required to provide details of the costs and benefits of incremental levels of service for each main activity, starting from zero and working up to present service levels and even beyond if required. The system also demands that each activity is ranked in order of the manager's perception of its priority. This information on service levels and priorities is then reviewed at successively higher levels of management, who would make their own recommendations on service levels and priorities, until the top executive review body makes the final decisions on which activities are to be retained and at what level of service they are to be pitched (either up or down).

Programme Planning and Budgeting System (PPBS)

PPBS while having broadly the same objectives as ZBB operates on a 'top down' basis whereby considerable emphasis is placed by top management on clearly defining policy objectives and priorities before specific service levels and operational targets are determined. One other feature which distinguishes it from other budgeting systems, including ZBB, is that budgets are developed for specific programmes and policy priorities rather than units, departments or services. PPBS facilitates a 'corporate' approach to budgeting since its preparation cuts across departmental boundaries and tends to highlight overlaps, duplications and contradictions in the conventional budget. The method also ensures that a time horizon for the budget can be tied to the proposed life of the programme rather than the somewhat arbitrary period of the financial year.

The accountability by programme which is an essential part of PPBS is designed to encourage several things, including:

1) Identifying the public's needs clearly and specifying precisely how they will be met.
2) Providing an objective basis for deciding the funding level for programmes and the priority in which they should be financed.
3) Describing how a particular programme will be organised and operated so that its efficiency can be assessed.

It should be stressed that PPBS, or for that matter ZBB, are not necessarily meant to replace the preparation of detailed line budgets nor to remove cost based reviews. On the contrary the cost based review process should complement these systems and provide the means of delivering reductions in cost, which can often be identified and targeted during the budget process.

Both PPBS and ZBB can provide a sound basis for informing the elected representatives and their electorate of the likely consequences of implementing policy decisions.

A Practical Approach

Two points should be appreciated in considering systems such as ZBB and PPBS. Firstly, they entail a considerable investment in time for all levels of management, much more so than conventional systems. In many public sector organisations their application may be a waste of time particularly in organisations such as water undertakings where the expenditure is driven more by demand than by political choice. In other words a water authority cannot stop supplying water for two days per week to save money and if land becomes flooded it has to be pumped dry.

A local authority on the other hand, has more political choice. It can, for example, close half its libraries on Mondays and Wednesdays to cut costs. The use of budgetary control therefore is a more flexible tool in the hands of the local authority whereas in the case of the water authority or similar public utility other techniques such as performance measurement may be of greater value.

The second point is that systems such as ZBB and PPBS have had a very chequered career, largely because financial management has not always been able to sell these complex and somewhat unpopular systems to their operational colleagues and the systems have been resisted. Many people will have read about the ill-fated attempts to introduce ZBB into the State of Georgia when Governor Carter was in office and the problems encountered by the US Defense Department in managing a PPBS project.

The secret in using these techniques would seem to be, if indeed the scope for their application exists in the first place, to accept that they are fairly theoretical and complex in conception and that only the bare practical essentials should be selected, as appropriate to the size and nature of the undertaking. The essence of these systems is to provide a critical appraisal of programmes and service levels to ensure, on the one hand that wagon wheels will not be produced into the 21st century and on the other that citizens' justifiable needs are being met efficiently.

The Use of Technology

Finally, a mention should be made of the use of technology in the preparation of budgets. Many authorities are making use of general ledger packages which provide the opportunity for on-line interpretation of selected budget and actual expenditure information. Certain of these packages offer facilities for the calculation of unit costs which can facilitate the use of comparative performance measures and targets. Mostly however, these systems are driven by large main-frame computers in the hands of central departments and considerable scope remains for the use of distributed micro-computers by politicians and management in service departments.

For example, everyone in local government is familiar with the frantic period during which the budgets are finalised and yet relatively little use is made of technology by those responsible for evaluating varying policy options. Considerable time and loss of temper could be saved if micro-computers were programmed for rapidly answering politicians' 'what ifs' such as 'what would be the effect of a 10% increase in swimming charges and a 3% drop in attendance?', or at a higher level 'what saving on Social

Services and Education administration costs would be required to allow a 1% saving on the general rate levies?' While some micro-computer packages have been developed in this area they are mostly, it appears, used by accountants. Their real benefit would be in the committee rooms to help politicians to reach more timely and informed decisions.

The use of micro-computer packages of this type would be of particular benefit in the operation of techniques such as ZBB where the incremental effect of different service levels needs to be calculated over a very wide range of activities.

Conclusion

In conclusion, it is clear that the use of such techniques as PPBS and ZBB and the introduction of technology such as interactive micro-computer systems is a very heady brew for many public sector organisations. While some organisations have attempted to introduce scientific methods of budgeting, such as the UK's Department for the Environment through its use of the Management Information for Ministers System (MINIS) all too many rely on the 'licence to spend money' approach to budgeting which in today's economic climate is an anachronism. Indeed many public sector organisations have not even got sufficiently accurate and equitable accounting systems in place to provide a firm foundation for even the simplest budgeting system. For example, many line managers are asked to take responsibility for items on their budget statements over which they have not the slightest control, for example, those large, and often unexplained, lumps of 'central overhead' which relate not to them but to the authority as a whole. Therefore, before the more advanced techniques can be considered the public sector organisation must seriously review its bread and butter accounting systems to see whether or not they are adequate to support better budgetary practice.

9 Rewards and Incentives for Good Value for Money

'It would be an unnerving thought for the would-be saver that if anything goes wrong there will be many people willing to trace a connection, however tenuous, with those economies about which as everybody knows, in their greater wisdom, they expressed doubts at the time.'

Leslie Chapman

As we mentioned earlier, large economies are to be found in the public sector if management and staff are properly motivated to search them out. Unfortunately, the ethos and culture of the public sector does not generally encourage a determined search for savings; rather the reverse, many public sector organisations are swept along by the apparently irresistible mechanism for spending a greater amount of money each year to maintain or enhance standards which may or may not be justified. The success of civil servants and local government officers is certainly not judged on their performance in the value for money field.

Until it is established that economising in all ways is something that public servants should be doing constantly as a matter of course, and until they are rewarded on that basis, real break-throughs in combating large scale waste will not occur. After all, politicians, consultants and other outside agencies such as external auditors, can act only as catalysts for change. It is the people in the front line who really understand the activities for which they are responsible and who should provide the most fruitful source of ideas for savings.

Recognition of Achievement

If significant inroads are therefore to be made into waste and extravagance then the present 'play for safety' attitudes prevalent in many public sector organisations must be replaced. The criteria used for appraising the performance of officials must include ability to achieve value for money and this should become an important consideration in assessing an official's career prospects. Indeed, the absence of a positive attitude to achieving value for money, whether in respect of economy, efficiency or effectiveness, should put a question mark against the official's suitability for promotion. These proposals would require a profound 'sea change' in the staff appraisal procedure of many public sector organisations which are slanted more to an official's ability to 'get on' with colleagues and superiors than for his ability to initiate change.

At present there is often an automatic progression through salary increments up to the maximum for a particular grade, particularly at the lower levels. We believe that the practice should be adopted of only giving increments to those recommended on some tangible evidence of achievement. Most enterprising people would like to feel they have been awarded their increments as a result of objectives achieved rather than having them given routinely for safe but uninspired service. The objectives themselves would of course not solely relate to value for money. However, changes which led to economies without impairing agreed service levels or changes which resulted in improved services at no extra cost should rate high in the assessment criteria.

Bonus Schemes

A more radical method of rewarding management for exceptional achievement would be to introduce a bonus scheme. Such schemes are used successfully and widely in the private sector but have found little favour in the public sector except for staff operating at a relatively low level.

At management level we have seen little evidence of such schemes although it is understood that the Audit Commission for Local Authorities in England and Wales has successfully introduced a management incentive scheme.

Certainly, there are major difficulties to be ironed out before a scheme could be introduced. While the profit factor in the private sector provides a fairly clear cut yardstick, measurement of performance, especially in 'soft' areas such as Social Services is still in the pioneering stage. Undoubtedly, an initiative as novel as incentive schemes needs the right background situation, the courage and willingness to take risks and above all a strong lead from the top. Nevertheless, while success is difficult to achieve in this area, and many mistakes are likely to be made en route, the rewards to be derived from an effective management incentive scheme could be well worth the effort involved.

Under such a scheme the basic salary for each grade might be supplemented by an annual bonus based upon performance for the year. The evaluation of performance would inevitably be partly subjective but also based upon factors such as achievement of targets, budgets, and service objectives, exceptional effort (such as carrying out the work of two posts) or for special contributions, eg material cost saving innovations. We would see the appraisal as being based upon a simple grading of say 4 or 5 performance categories with a bonus percentage being linked to each of the categories. This type of system has been used in a wide range of private sector organisations and certain public sector organisations. A fairly straightforward system for the public sector recommended by the Institute of Personnel Management for merit pay is based on five levels of performance as follows:

Excellent − 10%
Very effective − 7½%
Satisfactory − 5%
Barely satisfactory − 2½%
Unsatisfactory − 0%

Incentive schemes of this nature need to rely upon clear cut objectives and targets being set for each manager and for these to be backed by an accurate performance measurement system. The incentive scheme therefore has to be an integral part of the organisation's budgetary control and management information systems and linked of course to a suitable appraisal scheme. There are many other books which deal in detail with management performance and appraisal systems which is a subject outside the scope of this chapter; however, the main steps in maintaining an incentive scheme in, for example, a local government authority, might be as follows:

1) *Review critically service levels* − for each activity under scrutiny as part of the overall budget process. Identify and agree changes to standards and convert these to specific objectives to be achieved by the manager responsible expressed as quantifiable targets (eg reduce grass cuts on selected open spaces by 50%).
2) *Examine critically major cost headings* − and isolate areas for improvements in economy and efficiency as part of rolling cost based review process. Convert cost reduction opportunities to specific objectives to be achieved by the manager concerned (eg reduce energy costs by 10% for selected buildings).
3) *Identify opportunities for improving effectiveness* − on activities where planned objectives are not being met through the use of effectiveness measures such as consumer surveys and complaint registers. Convert these opportunities to specific targets to be met by the manager responsible (eg increase occupancy rate in selected homes for the aged by 15%).
4) *Prepare schedule of quantified targets* − for achievement by individual managers in agreement with them.
5) *Compare actual achievement with target objectives* − at the end of the year.
6) *Carry out appraisal process* − based on measured achievement together with subjective judgement of superiors on less quantifiable criteria (eg co-operation, application etc) and agree bonus percentage.

In the first instance the percentage bonus would be recommended by a manager's departmental head. In the circumstances it would be prudent for the recommendation to be reviewed by an independent body such as the performance review committee in a local authority. Otherwise there may be a danger of savings in one area (say Finance) being to the detriment of another (say Social Services). Also the independent committee should filter out undue bias by departmental management.

Removing Disincentives

As we have stressed, the types of incentive scheme we have discussed, whereby promotion, increments or bonuses are based on a system which takes account of properly measured value for money achievements have their dangers. However, there is no doubt that they would encourage managers with the right attitude of mind to achieve far more than is possible under the normal systems of reward in the public sector. However, not all inducements to achieving better value for money are related to direct benefits of this kind. A great deal needs to be done to remove other demotivating factors which are inherent in the present public sector organisation.

In particular the present 'annualised' system of budgeting (what Leslie Chapman calls the 'end of financial year madness'), needs to be removed. A great many people both in central and local government are encouraged to spend any spare money available at the year end quite often on totally unnecessary projects so that the money is not left 'unspent'. The budgeting process has to be flexible to allow managers to benefit from the savings they have achieved, either by allowing them to carry underspent balances forward to the following year, or to invest the money in areas which will enhance value for money in the longer term eg. energy conservation officers, O & M specialists, energy monitoring devices or micro-processors with which to reduce clerical work.

At present in most public sector organisations the budgetary process tends to be extremely inflexible and acts as a disincentive to achieving value for money. We quoted the instance earlier of the managers in a leisure services department, always a prime target for cuts, working hard to make savings throughout the year only to see the benefit of those savings swallowed up in other departments who may have better bargaining power at the committee tables.

Finally, it should be remembered that incentives to achieve good value for money should not only relate to the higher levels of management but some form of incentive should operate at every level of the organisation. A number of authorities, for example Welwyn Hatfield District Council, have introduced staff incentive schemes which have showed useful increases in productivity. Welwyn Hatfield claim that output has increased by about 9% over a 4½ year period but that current salary equivalents are down to the same level as 1978. In addition overtime payments are down by 17%. Also properly administered suggestion schemes which offer real incentives should be introduced. The people carrying out the work at the sharp end will respond admirably in producing cost saving ideas if they are given the right incentives and encouragement. Remember the example of the chargehand/electrician who saved £40,000 per annum by suggesting that gas cookers in the RAF mess kitchens were in future turned off when not in use!

10 The Economics of Contracting Out

'Tightened local government spending patterns have contributed to the need for innovative approaches to providing|services for local taxpayers. Contracting services to businesses,|neighbourhoods and nonprofit organisations is one of those approaches.'

John Tapper Marlin, President,
US Council on Municipal Performances

In a free market society the public sector should generally only be in the business of providing services which are not freely available elsewhere. In practice this is not the case and many opportunities exist for obtaining savings by transferring services from the public to the private sector. This chapter examines some of these opportunities, considers some of the pitfalls and attempts to provide practical advice on the methods of evaluating, and tendering for, services from the private sector. In doing so we intend to explore only the area of 'contracting out' of services as opposed to the privatisation of services. 'Contracting out' is the term used to describe the situation where an outside party is hired to carry out the work involved in providing a service but overall control of standards and accountability to the public remain with the authority. 'Privatisation' implies the selling off lock, stock and barrel of the service to the private sector (eg British Telecom) which is a political decision and outside the scope of this book.

Moves to contract out various sections of the public sector were underway before the present UK government's conservative administration came to power. However, it is true to say that moves to expand both the scope and pace of privatisation have been greatly accelerated by the present government's 'free market' ideology. As Boyle and Rich state:

Such has been the enthusiasm for the 'free marketeers' that Ministers covering the whole spectrum of government activity have considered 'privatising practically everything that is run by the State short of the Falklands Task Force'. Thus when asked what would be left to sell at the end of a third term for Mrs Thatcher, John Moore, Minister of State at the Treasury, replied 'The Treasury'.

Increasingly, local and health authorities have been under pressure to consider the possibility of letting out contracts for the provision of certain of their services in an attempt to improve value for money. For example, the UK Local Government Planning and Land Act 1980 allows local authorities to employ their direct labour organisations for work over certain limits only after competitive tender. In the specialised field of highway construction and maintenance, therefore, such bodies have now developed considerable experience of contracting out. In September 1983, the Department of Health and Social Security in the UK issued a circular requiring health authorities to prepare plans by February 1984 for the contracting out of domestic, catering and laundry services, and to consider the possibility of contracting out other activities.

While we are concerned here to concentrate on contracting out it is interesting that E. S. Savas in his book on the 'Comparative costs of public and private enterprise in a municipal service' distinguished eight alternatives to the direct production of services in the public sector. These are: inter-governmental contracting; contracting with the private sector; the award of franchises; the payment of grants to private suppliers; the distribution of vouchers to consumers; private purchases by consumers; supply through voluntary arrangements and self-service by consumers. Figure 10.1 provides a list of possible practical applications against each of these alternatives. In considering specifically the contracting out option, management should primarily decide on the basis of two criteria only: cost and efficiency. Whilst it is true that, on the one hand, public sector employees and their unions will resist such moves and that, on the other hand, private sector interests will lobby in the opposite direction for increased business, such conflicts should be regarded as being of only secondary importance, and entering the realms of ideology. Regrettably, many decisions to contract out, or indeed not to contract out, have been based on political motives rather than hard facts.

FIGURE 10.1   *Alternatives to the direct public sector*
provision of services

Alternative	Application
(a) Inter-governmental contracting	Computer services provided by one agency or department to another; a local authority parks department maintaining the grounds of a health authority.
(b) Private sector contracts	Laundering; building maintenance; cleaning; contract hire of vehicles.
(c) Franchises	Catering; printing; advertising
(d) Consumer vouchers	For accommodation, meals and transport.
(f) Private purchases by consumers	When brand-named medicines are preferred to generic-named alternatives.
(g) Supply through voluntary arrangements	Different to (d) above when, for example, sheltered housing is provided and entirely funded by charities and religious communities.
(h) Self-service by consumers	When, for example, a health authority suspends the use of its ambulances in collecting out-patients for hospital or clinic treatment. In such circumstances the consumer must meet this cost himself.

It is also unfortunate that evidence on the relative efficiency of public and private production is extremely limited. To quote from Neald ('Public Expenditure'):

> The combination of little evidence and acute ideological significance makes for a heady brew: universal generalisations are drawn on the basis of a few empirical studies and the impressionistic examples.

While therefore dramatic savings have been claimed for contracting out, often the actual cases do not bear too close a financial scrutiny. In some instances the important 'non-avoidable' costs have not been taken into account such as inspection and central overheads. In 1980 the British Civil Service in justifying a decision to privatise 11,000 jobs in such areas as building supplies, maintenance and cleaning, stated in a memorandum to the Treasury and Civil Service Committee that they were unable to quantify the net, as opposed to gross cost. There are therefore few well documented case histories for use by authorities considering contracting out and while no one would dispute that significant savings can be made, authorities need to ensure that their evaluations are based on well considered facts and not on emotions. A selection from such reasonably well documented cases of contracting out as do exist in both the health and local government areas are shown at the end of this chapter.

A further problem in making a fair comparison is that of government interference. All too often public sector bodies have been used as vehicles for policies such as regional development, employment maintenance and support for domestic industries through purchasing directives; policies which have sometimes inhibited good management practice. For example, government directives to central government departments to support the British computer industry, through ordering only from International Computers Limited (ICL), led to three problems: more competitive prices could not be accepted; the variety of equipment was restricted and long delays in delivery were experienced. Such policies imposed by central government inevitably contribute to departments failing to pursue efficiency and hence automatically to appear less attractive than a potential private sector competitor.

However, whilst it may be true that direct comparisons between public and private sector provision of services are difficult, for whatever reason, the fact remains that there will be continuing pressure from government for public sector agencies to compare the costs of various parts of their services with outside tenders. If previous policies have disadvantaged a particular service it cannot be allowed to remain uncompetitive. Efforts should be made to see how potential improvements/savings could enhance the service efficiency before comparisons can fairly be made with private sector alternatives.

Advantages and Disadvantages of Contracting Out

Having considered the present impetus for contracting out various public sector services to the private sector and having discussed some of the complications that underlie such decisions, it is perhaps useful to summarise the advantages and disadvantages of contracting out.

Advantages:

1) The primary advantage of contracting out services should be cash savings or increased capacity of service.
2) Flexibility of operations (eg less restrictive practices).
3) Performance reviews can become less sensitive and more selective.

There are three potential sources of savings that allow private contractors to undercut in-house services. They are the rational use of labour, freedom from capital budget constraints, and economies of scale. The use of a contractor often eliminates entrenched restrictive practices and out-dated terms of service. Contractors do not have the same capital budget constraints as their public sector counterparts, consequently they have the ability to adopt new technology at a faster pace and hence to both improve their service and save on costs. The third of these factors will only be important if the public sector unit is comparatively small.

Disadvantages:

1) Future price increases beyond those had the service remained in-house and the consequent difficulties associated with reverting to a public sector service.
2) Risk of poor performance.
3) A lack of management expertise in effectively administering the tendering procedure.

A major fear of management is that once a decision has been made to contract out a service there can be little possibility of reversing the process should the need arise. It is not unknown for an organisation to have sold the capital equipment associated with a particular service, often to the contractor, and it could therefore lack the financial reserves necessary to re-establish the service in-house. To counteract the possibility of poor performance, management must ensure that there are sufficient options available to them to fully redress the situation with the contractor. A common effect when contracting out services is the failure to retain good functional managers who can provide a high level of supervision. Management are still needed to monitor performance and quality control, and they should have time to consider the future direction of the service. The widespread use of contracted out services will end job security and threaten the existence of restrictive practices so resulting in industrial relations problems. Often contracted out services use lower levels of manpower and employees receive lower rates of pay.

A further disadvantage which is also important is that if individual departments or service centres do not receive, even in part, some of the potential savings, then the system actually discourages management initiative.

What Services should be considered?

A wide range of public sector activities can be considered for contracting out to the private sector. As a general guide, the following list of characteristics can help identify areas that management might consider as having potential for contracting out:

- capital or labour intensive;
- partially contracted to the private sector or partially or wholly contracted out to other public sector bodies;
- joint/shared responsibility with public, private or voluntary body;
- self-contained activities;
- commercial or quasi-commercial activity;
- seasonal activity;
- definable and measurable levels of performance;
- lack of capacity for present/anticipated service demand;
- change in method/practice.

Within these broad areas specific services which local government and health authorities have, to date, contracted out to the private sector include the following:

Cleaning; Laundering; Maintenance of Buildings, Plant and Equipment; Car Parking; Refuse Collection and Waste Disposal; Purchasing and Supplies; Sheltered Housing; Transport; Catering; Advertising and Publicity; Recruitment and Training; Management Services; Estate Management; Security.

This list is not exhaustive, merely illustrative of the services presently undertaken for public bodies by private sector businesses in the UK.

Preparation and Evaluation of Tenders

As we have already implied, great care must be taken when seeking competitive tenders for contracting out a service to the private sector to safeguard the longer term interests of an authority, not only in response to the financial aspects but in terms of quality of service. The object of the exercise should be to obtain a stipulated standard of service for the best possible price. As such the tender document should:

1) Clearly define the characteristics and level of service required and
2) Request information in such a way as to facilitate the comparison of one tender with another (including one prepared for the retention of the service in-house).

In our experience most tenders tend to be specific as to service provision. Sometimes however, public sector bodies have produced very general tender specifications that only state the desired results and leave the contractor to determine how best these objectives are to be met. This is a dangerous practice and can lead to an erosion of standards even though savings may be achieved. Generally speaking the public sector body is best placed to determine the exact specifications of its service requirement and potential contractors prefer this approach. Appendices to each detailed tender specification should therefore provide a schedule of activities required. The appropriate limit(s) of activity should be defined and the total quantity(ies) of unit(s) per period identified. A variation to this approach is to prepare tenders in which two or three different levels of service are suggested. In this way the marginal cost of, say, emptying dustbins twice a week rather than once a week can be established and the cost of the second collection weighed against its benefits at the evaluation stage.

As a general rule all tender documents should clearly state the definition of terms and responsibilities (as necessary), legal liabilities, terms of payment, tax matters and so on. Penalties should be clearly stated. Many public sector bodies now require the contractor to deposit a 'Performance Bond' with themselves or a third party. In case of default, the hirer can simply liquidate the bond in order to seek compensation. If the contractor is a subsidiary of a parent company the contractor should be required to submit a deed of guarantee by which the parent company indemnifies the authority against losses, damages, costs and expenses arising as a result of any defaulting on the contract by the subsidiary firm.

Tender documentation must clearly state how price fluctuations due to inflation are to be dealt with. Generally speaking either a published index is used; for example, the Retail Price Index, or, alternatively the public sector body negotiates with the contractor as to what agreed price fluctuations can be implemented on stated review dates. Such measures are necessary in order to ensure that the price changes claimed by the contractor are fair and reasonable. Earlier it was stated that one consequence of contracting out services was that the wages and salaries element of the tender may well be lower than that paid in-house. One reason for this was the repeal, in 1983, of the 'Fair Wages Resolution 1946'. Since that time the requirements of the resolution have not been included in Government contracts and guidance has been issued that suggests that local and health authorities should do likewise. Such a suggestion remains, for the moment, a matter for each authority's individual discretion.

The Chartered Institute of Public Finance and Accountancy further suggests that each contractor be required to submit two certificates. The first to certify that there has been no collusion with other potential contractors, the second to certify that there was no in-house favouritism shown to the contractor.

Most public sector bodies have a list of approved contractors whom they invite to tender. One method of establishing such a list would be to issue to those who wish to apply a pre-qualification questionnaire. An approved list is usually preferred because it considerably reduces the work that would otherwise ensue if the tender was open. Details of how tenders are to be submitted are defined in the tender documentation.

Correct Use of Costs

Those charged with preparing the in-house tender should not be misled by any existing accounts and budgets relating to the service in question. Past costs are irrelevant; it is future opportunity costs that are relevant. In other words, the in-house team must estimate, as accurately as possible, what costs would be avoided by the public sector body if the in-house service ceased. Arbitrary allocations of overheads must not be included since their incidence will continue regardless of whether the service is contracted out.

Only direct current costs are relevant. Historic based figures are useless and irrelevant. Most public sector bodies fail to adequately record the capital cost of their assets. For the purposes of the tender it is the annual equivalent of the actual value of the assets that should enter the tender costing. For example, if a transport authority presently owned a fleet of buses their cost in the tender should be based on their value from present use. One approach would be to estimate the value of the fleet at the start of the contract and offset this by the cost of the suitably discounted residual fleet value at the end of the period. The question of what discount rate is used is a complicated one and readers are advised to take expert advice. As a general guideline, weighted average cost of capital should be used. One that is (1) weighted by the current market value of capital employed by the organisation and (2) uses marginal/future predicted interest dates.

In evaluating tenders the first consideration is the capability and technical resources of the potential contractors. It may be advisable to interview the short-listed contractors. Once this stage has been finalised a fair financial evaluation of the tenders should be made.

Transitional Arrangements

The transitional period between the awarding of a contract and its commencement date will normally be a period of intense activity for an authority. The work involved relates to two main areas of concern: termination of the existing in-house provision and the start of the contractor's operations. One of the most important aspects of terminating the in-house provision is the negotiations with existing staff who are to be made redundant at the commencement date of the contract. The provision of redundancy payments in the UK is a complex matter and legal advice will need to be sought in interpreting Section 81 of the Employment Protection (Consolidation) Act 1978 as it applies to particular cases.

The other major tasks associated with the implementation of the contract include discussions with the contractor and the establishment of the machinery necessary to manage the contract after implementation. It is important that a good working relationship is established between an authority and the contractor's representative who should have a detailed knowledge of the authority's requirements before operations start.

In setting up the machinery for supervising and managing a contract, particular attention will need to be paid to the setting up of suitable systems for financial control, financial reporting and performance monitoring.

An authority should also ensure that a contractor provides any deed of guarantee, performance bond and certificates of insurance required under the terms of the contract. If the contractor fails to produce evidence of sufficient insurance, the employing authority may have to pay the insurance itself, deducting that sum from any monies due to the contractor. This situation would only arise however where the risk would fall on the authority rather than the contractor.

In some authorities the question of insurance may not arise as in the case of Health Authorities who do not insure certain risks where the assets are dispersed to such a degree that insurance is not cost justified.

Supervision of Contracts

Management must have sufficient resources to oversee the operation of the contract. The effective management of contracts after letting is by no means a soft option. Laing ('Contracting out in the National Health Service') discusses this point in relation to the National Health Service. For example, he states:

. . .Catering used to be quite commonly contracted out, but because of lackadaisical management, such contracts fell into disrepute. If contracting out is to be more successful in the future, it will have to be seen as an opportunity for managers to apply performance indicators and tighter quality control, and to focus on broader management issues at the same time. Some administrations feel that the Service is capable of this, others have doubts. There are parallel doubts about the ability of private contractors to deliver what they promise. In an effort to demonstrate a new and professional approach, model contracts for laundry and catering services have been developed by trade associations. But contracting out on a large scale remains a relatively unknown quantity.

Often the observing of quality standards say in the case of refuse collection means no more than carefully logging and dealing with complaints made by the public on such issues as non-collections of refuse and the leaving of litter in the refuse area. Tamworth Borough Council, for example, kept a detailed record of the number and type of complaints arising from the refuse service both before and after it had been contracted out. In this case they reported a falling off in the rate of complaints under the private service. Other authorities have not been so lucky. Certain authorities have however felt it necessary to introduce more searching quality control methods such as the use of consumer surveys. These surveys have been employed successfully in the USA and Canada, notably by the City of Thunder Bay in Ontario who carry out consumer surveys in a number of areas such as road maintenance, refuse collection and parks and recreation. As we have said elsewhere in this book, consumer surveys have to be carefully thought out and planned and above all questions have to be framed without bias, political or otherwise. An extract from a well balanced and bias free survey questionnaire drawn up by the Recreation Department of the District of Columbia is shown as Figure 10.2 to this chapter. It also has to be borne in mind that interview type surveys can be expensive although often sample sizes of 200/300 people can be adequate and can in certain instances be carried out by telephone. Should the need arise, due

FIGURE 10.2

Q3. How would you or your household members rate the facilities that you have used during the past month?

Facility Name	Characteristics	Very Good	Good	Fair	Poor	Don't Know
(a)	i) Hours of Operation					
	ii) Cleanliness					
	iii) Condition of Equipment					
	iv) Helpfulness and Attitude of Personnel					
	v) Amount of Space					
	vi) Safety					
	vii) Overall Rating					

[The above question was asked about each facility that had been used by the household. It provides evaluation of various quality characteristics]

Q4. Would you give me the reasons why during the last months your household did not use the following facilities?

READ REASONS. INDICATE RESPONSE BY CHECK MARK IN BOX.

	Names of Facilities		
a. Don't know about facility or its programs			
b. Not open the right times			
c. Too far away			
d. Too crowded			
e. Not attractive			
f. Costs too much to go there			
g. Too dangerous there			
h. Do not like other users			
i. Personal health			
j. Activities not interesting IF CHECKED ASK WHAT WOULD BE INTERESTING			
k. Too busy			
l. Other (SPECIFY)			

Source: "Obtaining Citizen Feedback", The Urban Institute.

to the contractor defaulting on the level of service required, contingency arrangements will have to be made. This brings to mind the sad story of Dacorum District Council which signed a three year contract for catering at the council's pavilion.

After six months the contractor announced he would be withdrawing, giving the council less than three weeks' notice to mount a rescue operation. It is now running the catering itself. Defaulting in cases like this will either involve bringing in another contractor or providing the service on an in-house basis, at least for an interim period. This may necessitate the public sector body recovering or taking over certain capital assets and staff currently employed by the contractor. Once a replacement service has been established, legal action should be taken against the defaulting contractor in order to recover any losses. Normally, however, the contract will last for the length of the agreement. At such time the authority will then have to decide whether to extend the existing contract for a further fixed period or put the service out to tender again.

Contracting Out in the Health Service

The National Health Service in England and Wales has been fairly active in the use of outside contractors and some lessons can be learned from their experience.

Figure 10.3 provides an indication of the variety of services contracted out. Perhaps the most surprising aspect of this table is the contracting out of certain operations to the growing number of private hospitals. For example, hip operations have been contracted out as a way of dealing with a temporary lack of facilities or a short term excess of demand. In fact the process of tendering can have surprising spin-offs. The South West Thames region temporarily contracted out hip replacements to the private sector and, by investigating its own services at the same time, found that it could substantially improve in-house efficiency.

At the time of writing, at least nine district health authorities have refused to follow the Social Services Secretary's order to submit timetables so that cleaning, catering and laundry services go out to tender before the September 1986 deadline. On the other hand Bromley District Health Authority has awarded several

FIGURE 10.3 *Hospital and Community Services Contracted Out*

	Total revenue expenditure	External contracts	
	£m	£m	% of total
Total, all services	6,551	163	2.5
Patient care	4,037	45	1.1
Homes and hospitals	—	27	—
Maintenance of technical equipment	—	18	—
General services	2,216	118	5.3
Catering	316	1	0.3
Portering	126	0	0.0
Domestic/cleaning	375	10	2.6
Linen/laundry	146*	7	4.8
Transport	30*	7	23.0
Estate management	637*	93	15.0
Other	586	—	—
Other, including ambulance	298	0	0.0

* Hospitals only.

Sources: NHS Appropriations Accounts; Second Report from the Social Services Committee, session 1981/82, Vol II.

domestic contracts to private contractors. Figure 10.4 provides further recent illustrations of the contracts awarded to private sector firms, together with projected annual savings.

Health authorities such as Bromley have experienced initial teething problems but the management now consider that there is no difference in quality between in-house and outside cleaners. Other districts, such as North Staffordshire admit to not fully being able to quantify the benefits, financial and otherwise, from

FIGURE 10.4   *Illustrative Examples of Contracted Out Services in the National Health Service*

Health Authority	Service	Company	Annual saving
Bromley	Domestic cleaning	ISS Hospital Service	*
	Hospital cleaning	Hospital Hygiene Services	£400,000
Camberwell	Laundry	Sunlight	£56,000
Croydon	Laundry	Advance	*
East Surrey	Hospital domestic services	Crothall	£50,000
	Laundry	AE Chapman	£100,000
Gwent	Staff transport (buses)	Hills of Tredegar	£23,251
Huntingdon	Domestic services	Lesters	£200,000
Kingston and Esher	Laundry	Advance	*
Maidstone	Laundry	Smarts	£35,000
Medway	Hospital domestic services	Exclusive	£357,184
Merton and Sutton	Laundry	Advance	£90,000
Milton Keynes	Hospital domestic services	Crothall	*
North Warwickshire	Laundry	Initial	£70,000
North West Surrey	Laundry	Initial	£210,000
South Derbyshire	Steam heat for boilers	Associated Heat Services	£30,000
Surrey	Street cleaning	Exclusive	£12,000

*Authority unwilling to give figures.

Source: Accountancy Age, 18 October 1984.

their privatisation programmes. There are also districts, such as Cheltenham, where the National Union of Public Employees claim that only 15% of contracted out laundry met the required quality-control standards. Under continuing government pressure the health authorities will have to open up their ancillary services to competitive tendering whether they like it or not. Similar moves have been made in the areas of local government. All the signs are that this impetus will increase. As such, management should evaluate these possibilities with an open mind and consider both the quality of service and the potential for cash savings.

Local Authority Contracting Out Experience

A considerable number of contracting out exercises have been carried out in the local government area in the UK. While the most popular topics have been office cleaning, street sweeping, toilet cleaning and refuse collection, a very wide diversity of other services have been contracted out to the private sector, including such not immediately obvious areas as gulley emptying, traffic signal maintenance, crematorium maintenance, sports injury treatment and sauna and solarium management. The last example, could perhaps prompt the question, what are local government doing running facilities such as these anyway? Many would argue such services are best left to the private sector. Figure 10.5 provides a range of examples of the savings which have directly resulted from contracting out.

Two particularly interesting trends are apparent from our review of contracted out work in local government. Firstly, that contracting out has not always been geared towards financial savings – councils are also looking to improve the quality of services. For example, Broadlands District Council awarded a £7,000 contract for outside caterers to run the council's staff restaurant with the aim of providing a better standard of catering. Similarly Essex CC is running a pilot scheme with contractors on school meals catering even though this is costing more than the in-house service.

The other trend is that the threat of contracting out has acted as a powerful catalyst for savings. A survey carried out by the Local Government Chronicle in June 1983 showed that five authorities gained savings of more than £½ million per year through voluntary revisions of the refuse collection manning levels in the face of tenders from private operators. In a recent contracting out study we carried out on refuse collection for a Metropolitan Borough Council the work force came up with proposals which undercut

FIGURE 10.5

Authority	Political control	Service contracted out	Annual saving
Metropolitan Districts			
Wirral	Conservative	Refuse collection/street cleaning and maintenance/ operations of public conveniences	£700,000 in 83/4.⎤£1.4m in full year.
Croydon	Conservative	1. Library bindery 2. Public conveniences	1. £22,000 2. £76,000
Merton	Conservative	Refuse collection/ street cleaning/ waste paper recovery	£750,000
District Councils			
Babergh	NOC*	Jobbing housing repairs	£10,000
Bracknell	Conservative	Landscape maintenance	£10,000
Epping Forest	Conservative	Pest control	£2,000
Gedling	Conservative	Office cleaning	£12,000
Gloucester	Conservative	1. Horticultural produce 2. Cattle market cleansing	£24,000 £40,000
Mendip	Independent	Refuse collection	£611,000 over 5 years
Yeovil	NOC*	Office cleaning	£21,500
Waveney	Conservative	Golf course leased to private contractor	£2,000

*NOC = no overall control

Source: Local Government Chronicle, June 1983.

the tenders received from private contractors. The authority were delighted both to achieve savings, which in their case amounted to about £400,000 per year, and also to retain an excellent work force which has provided a first class service.

In their negotiations the in-house workforce insisted on two points as a condition to their saving a significant number of men and vehicles. Firstly they opted for a five year contract (this would have been given to the outside contractors), secondly they asked that supervisory and administration overheads were reduced in proportion to their savings. Both points were conceded by management.

Conclusion

In the face of reduced funding and resources, most public sector organisations have been seeking ways to reduce service costs and in many service areas private sector firms have performed as well as central or local government at less cost. Many public sector organisations who have exhausted internal cutback opportunities may find many more useful savings through contracting out. Even where there is not scope to contract out an entire activity or where, as in some European countries, there are strong political objections, staffing levels may often be reduced by using contractors to iron out the peaks in demand.

Part III Case Studies and Checklists

11 Improving Value for Money – Case Studies

This chapter provides several case studies of actual value for money reviews, selected because they each illustrate a particular feature of value for money work we wish to draw to the reader's attention and underline various important points in the book.

The first relating to a State Highway maintenance system in the USA has been taken from Richard Brown's 'Auditing performance in Government'. The remaining studies were carried out by Price Waterhouse, in all cases in close liaison with top management, both permanent officers and politicians.

The State Highway case is particularly interesting as it shows an imaginative approach to evaluating the effectiveness of programmes while at the same time relating service levels to the money spent, both by the state and by neighbouring authorities.

The case study relating to a large public utility underlines the opportunities for increasing administrative and clerical productivity, a somewhat neglected area.

As we have mentioned earlier considerable opportunities also exist for savings in the 'soft' areas such as social services and education especially in the non-operational fields. The case study on a social services department illustrates how savings of over £1 million per annum were made without disturbing the level of service provided by fieldworkers and other 'front line' staff. The review in social services was carried out alongside a review of an education department, which space precludes us from describing here, but which led to a similar scale of savings through better energy conservation and the contracting out of school and college cleaning.

We have also included a small Borough Council in the case studies, not because our review revealed enormous savings, but because the authority, subject to a few relatively minor improvements, provided a useful model for other small authorities in its review and monitoring arrangements for value for money.

The case study relating to a District Health Authority illustrates a successful example of an area where the public sector is often not particularly adroit, namely capital investment to achieve longer term gains. In this case the installation of 'cook-chill' catering when the anticipated payback would not take place for about two years.

Finally, the case study on refuse collection in a metropolitan borough shows how a work force voluntarily accepted a reduction in men and vehicles to undercut tenders received from outside contractors. Their rewards were better productivity bonuses and a five year contract.

IMPROVING VALUE FOR MONEY – CASE STUDY

State Highway Maintenance Programme

Objectives

1) How effectively does the state's highway maintenance programme provide safe, smooth and attractive highways that are
   maintained, as nearly as possible, like new?
2) How do the state's maintenance costs and services differ from
   those of surrounding states, and why?

Methods   To help to answer the question of how effectively the highways were maintained the reviewers hired a professional civil engineering consultant. The consultant analysed a sample of 12 state highways that crossed into bordering states using visual inspections, analysis of road surfaces and comparisons of agency records. The features considered included the appearance of rest areas and roadsites, the quality of repairing and resurfacing roads, shoulders and approaches, and the provision of safety measures such as signs and lighting. To supplement the consultant's findings the reviewers developed a survey that would show what citizens thought about the maintenance of their highways. A total of 283 people were interviewed by telephone.

To compare the state's maintenance costs with those of surrounding states, the reviewers spent a week in each of the four border states to better understand the maintenance systems in these states and to collect comparable data. Information on both total maintenance costs and 'unit' costs for maintenance services (eg cost per mile to maintain road surfaces) was collected and analysed.

Maintenance standards issued by the American Association of State Highway and Corporation Officers were used to judge the recorded levels of the type and costs of maintenance services.

Findings and results   The results of the 'effectiveness' part of the review are shown in table 11.1. As will be seen the consultants rating of conditions was good overall and was closely paralleled by the user survey ratings with one notable exception — road surfaces were generally considered to be too rough or uneven by the public. The main criticism by the consultant, with which the user survey agreed, was that road shoulders were in poor condition, namely that they were often too narrow, rough or steep. As a result of this finding it was recommended that the Department of Transportation should evaluate the cost of constructing and maintaining paved shoulders on all highways carrying more than 1,700 vehicles per day. The cost analysis part of the review showed that the state spent 43% more than comparable neighbouring states to maintain its highways. In particular, the state spent much more than the border states to protect its highway investment through maintenance of existing road surfaces, shoulders and bridges. For example, the state spent 937 dollars per mile to maintain its road surfaces, nearly 2½ times as much as surrounding states. Yet the state's road surfaces were in no better condition, and, in fact, had some deficiencies not noted in the road surfaces in other states. The state also spent twice as much as the other states to maintain its hard shoulders and bridges, even though its hard shoulders had several serious problems.

TABLE 11.1 Drivers' Opinions of State Highways, July 1978

Highway characteristic by Priority Area	Consultant's findings (as percent of new)	Citizens' Survey results			Major reason for dissatisfaction
		Drivers' opinion (percent)			
		Satisfied	Dissatisfied	No opinion	
Traffic control					
Snow and ice control	Not evaluated	70.8	10.2	19.0	Slow in clearing roads / Slippery spots after plowing
Highway signs	80	70.3	28.3	1.4	Missing or blocked from view; confusing / Various reasons
Pavement markings	80	74.9	23.0	2.1	Hard to see
Guardrails	90			Not evaluated	
Protection of investment					
Road surface	87	50.5	47.7	1.8	Road rough, bumpy, or uneven
Road shoulders	67	47.0	44.6	8.4	None or too narrow / Too rough or too steep / Various reasons
Bridges	83			Not evaluated	
Drainage	78			Not evaluated	
Appearance and environment					
Appearance (mowing, litter, landscaping)	83	71.4	28.2	0.4	Mowing; litter; landscaping / Advertising / Various responses

The reviewers discovered that costs were particularly high in this state for two major reasons: the state's extensive resurfacing programme and its lack of investment in labour saving equipment. After further investigation two major recommendations were made:

1) Expanding the department's road overlay programme to reduce patch and repairs costs. The overlaying method although initially more expensive would save money in the long run, because it would last three times as long and require less maintenance throughout the overlay's life.
2) Purchase more modern and labour saving equipment.

On the basis of these improvements it was recommended that the Department should develop a plan for reducing the size of its maintenance field staff by 370 persons at an annual saving of $3.8 million in wages costs and fringe benefits. Out of these savings the state could invest $1.2 million in modernising its equipment and the remaining $2.6 million to defray the initial costs of stepping up the overlay programme.

IMPROVING VALUE FOR MONEY – CASE STUDY

Improving Administrative Efficiency in a Large Public Utility

Objective   The senior management of a large public utility were concerned about the effectiveness and cost of its finance function. In particular, the relative size of the regional finance departments and their use of centralised computer systems were questioned.

Methods   Consultants from Price Waterhouse were called in and undertook an Administrative Audit in conjunction with a review of the accounting systems. Performance ratios relating to the number of transactions processed by finance staff were developed and evaluated for each regional department to quantify their relative performances. Comparisons were also made with the performance of departments engaged in similar activities in a number of other businesses including other public utilities, engineering and consumer product companies. In some cases it was demonstrated that even the most effective regions were not achieving an acceptable performance.

Examples of the ratios used include:

1) Number of invoices processed to number of finance staff
2) Annual capital expenditure to number of finance staff
3) Stock value to number of finance staff
4) Operating costs to number of finance staff.

Results   The Administrative Audit identified those areas where the performance of individual regions was significantly worse than that of other regions, and areas where the performance of all the regional departments compared unfavourably with the other businesses examined. The consultants then prepared an action plan designed to eliminate the factors causing poor results and to create a more effective finance function. This action plan set out short, medium and long term strategies, including improvements to the accounting systems which resulted in an immediate annual saving of £60,000, equal to 10% of the total staff cost.

IMPROVING VALUE FOR MONEY – CASE STUDY

Social Services Department of a large Metropolitan District Council

Objectives   The purpose of the exercise was to review the suitability of the organisation structure, systems and management information to meet the objectives of the department.

Methods   The methodology adopted in carrying out the review was as follows:

1) Discussions with the officers of the department
2) Examination and quantification of the data collected and work recorded
3) Comparisons with information from previous periods and locations
4) Reference to Government recommendations on matters relating to social services

5) Reference to committee policy and relevant legislation
6) Reference to reports produced by the department.

Results   The review produced a number of diverse recommendations which in total resulted in an annual cash saving of some £1.1 million net.

The main recommendations are summarised below:

1) The previous centralised structure was replaced with a decentralised structure based upon four districts each subdivided into areas.
2) A small central core of staff was retained consisting of the director and his personal staff, training section and domestic support section. In addition, the review recommended the establishment of a central inspectorate to monitor standards, progress towards objectives, and undertake research and planning functions.
3) In relation to fieldwork operations:
   (*a*) objectives and priorities to be clearly defined
   (*b*) greater emphasis to be placed on recording and monitoring the time spent by social workers on cases
   (*c*) the distribution of social workers to be revised and based on needs
   (*d*) the number of team leaders to be significantly reduced with some of their responsibilities taken over by area managers.
4) The care services division should be reorganised on a client group basis; child care, handicapped services, care of the elderly.
5) Staffing in the elderly persons' homes should be improved to a target staffing ratio of 1:8.
6) Posts in care services found to be duplicating the work of others should be deleted. In addition the allocation of clerical support should be revised to an equitable basis and excess posts deleted.
7) The department should begin to computerise its manual clerical systems. The cost of this programme should be more than offset by savings from the deletion of clerical posts.
8) The research, planning and development section should be deleted and its role taken over by the central inspectorate.

9) The purchasing and stores section together with the maintenance section should be deleted. Their work to be undertaken by other departments within the authority.

IMPROVING VALUE FOR MONEY – CASE STUDY

Small Borough Council

Objective   The Local Government Finance Act 1982 requires an authority's auditor to satisfy himself that suitable arrangements are in place to ensure economy, efficiency and effectiveness in the use of the authority's resources.

Methods and findings   The scope of the review covered two main aspects, namely:

1) An investigation of the organisational structure, control procedures and information systems used to secure VFM. This part of the review was carried out by discussion with chief officers and their staff and by reviewing appropriate documents, such as job specifications, budget statements and annual reports.
2) An analysis of the service costs of the authority. In this part of the review the Audit Commission 'profile' was used containing comparisons between the authority and the average costs for other district authorities with similar demographic characteristics (the 'family'). Costs were also compared with other selected authorities including one in particular with an almost identical population size and demographic characteristics (eg high percentage of young people and of unemployed).

The overall conclusion was that the authority had built a sound structural and procedural framework for achieving value for money. There was also a positive attitude on the part of management towards improving economy, efficiency and effectiveness which had resulted in a wide range of cost reduction innovations.

The authority's costs stood up very well by comparison to similar authorities. It also fell comfortably within the Governments's grant related expenditure targets. In most cases areas of apparent high spending could be identified as being due to high service provision (eg much greater acreage of open spaces per 1000 population than average), high levels of activity (eg the large number of development planning applications received) or high debt charges due to the relative newness of the housing stock and other facilities.

Results   The authority's cost containment record was set against an exceptional rise in population over the period 1971/82 (60%).

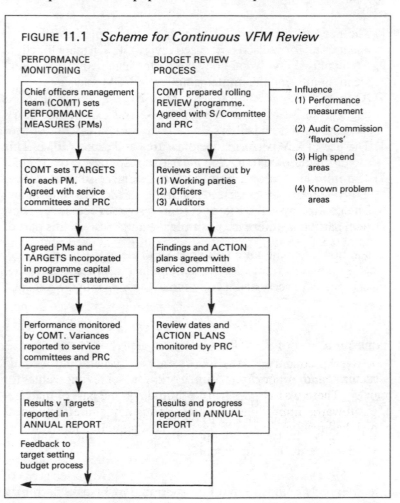

FIGURE 11.1   *Scheme for Continuous VFM Review*

PERFORMANCE MONITORING

Chief officers management team (COMT) sets PERFORMANCE MEASURES (PMs)

↓

COMT sets TARGETS for each PM. Agreed with service committees and PRC

↓

Agreed PMs and TARGETS incorporated in programme capital and BUDGET statement

↓

Performance monitored by COMT. Variances reported to service committees and PRC

↓

Results v Targets reported in ANNUAL REPORT

Feedback to target setting budget process

BUDGET REVIEW PROCESS

COMT prepared rolling REVIEW programme. Agreed with S/Committee and PRC

↓

Reviews carried out by
(1) Working parties
(2) Officers
(3) Auditors

↓

Findings and ACTION plans agreed with service committees

↓

Review dates and ACTION PLANS monitored by PRC

↓

Results and progress reported in ANNUAL REPORT

Influence
(1) Performance measurement

(2) Audit Commission 'flavours'

(3) High spend areas

(4) Known problem areas

This large rise in population and the accompanying demand for services brought the authority to the point where it was appropriate for the excellent foundations for VFM control to be co-ordinated and developed in a more formalised way. Accordingly, in liaison with the chief executive and the treasurer, a number of refinements to the present VFM arrangements were proposed. They provided a review and monitoring system which would be a useful model for other authorities of similar size. The main areas were:

1) The need to set an authority-wide strategic plan for the systematic and formalised cost based review of each main function.
2) An increased involvement by the performance review committee in monitoring the implementation of VFM measures.
3) A more co-ordinated approach to the use of the various elements engaged in VFM review, ie officers, and external auditors, working parties and others.
4) The use of key performance measures and targets to assist in monitoring productivity and the use of resources.
5) The introduction of a management incentive scheme to help motivate a keener interest in obtaining VFM.
6) The control over the use of certain resources requires review with particular reference to surplus land.

In addition a scheme for continuous VFM review was developed. This is shown in figure 11.1 and demonstrates the performance measurement process and its relation to the VFM review process.

IMPROVING VALUE FOR MONEY – CASE STUDY

District Health Authority

Objective   The objective of the review was to identify, evaluate and discuss the main cook-chill options available to the authority. Additionally, the review sought to highlight the salient points for consideration during implementation.

Methods and findings   One of the most important tasks during the review was the accumulation of relevant data for consideration and evaluation. This was achieved by:

1) Interviewing officers of the authority.
2) Reviewing relevant statistical and financial information generated by the authority.
3) Reviewing an internal exercise on cook-chill catering carried out by the authority.
4) Meeting representatives of equipment manufacturers and institutional catering concerns.

Cook-chill methods are used extensively in industry and on the continent. The main advantages over conventional methods are that, with proper management and control, significant staff savings can in certain circumstances be achieved by the adoption of production line methods. Also, quality of food at the point of consumption is improved, and ward staff have greater flexibility in arranging meal times.

The authority had already decided to go ahead and set up cook-chill catering facilities at its main hospital. However, the planned capacity of this new facility was such that with double shift working, all of the authority's establishments could be supplied.

The review therefore considered whether cook-chill catering should be confined to the main hospital or expanded to include some, or all, of the authority's remaining establishments.

Prior to examining cook-chill in detail however it was necessary to assess the effectiveness of the current catering arrangements. It was found that there were significant differences in the methods of operating at the various establishments within the authority. For example, certain units operated a bulk meals service while others operated a plated meals service. The plated meals service was said to be the more expensive method of the two. Another finding was that there were large variations in catering staff overtime payments.

Following the initial review of the current catering operations it seemed likely that cook-chill catering operations would yield significant savings. Most of the remaining work was therefore largely taken up with costing the alternative cook-chill options. The main factors to be taken into account included:

1) Location of establishments
2) Capacity of kitchen
3) Hardware costs including blast chillers
4) Staff implications
5) Back-up facilities in case of break-down etc
6) Operating factors such as serving, preparation of meals
7) Transportation of chilled meals
8) Food quality and wastage
9) Special diets.

Results   The main object of the review was to present the authority with a range of alternative options showing the financial implications of each. After extensive investigative work the objective was achieved and substantial savings were projected.

IMPROVING VALUE FOR MONEY − CASE STUDY

Metropolitan Borough

Objective   To carry out a review of manning levels, vehicle utilisation and levels of income for the refuse collection service for both commercial and domestic users.

Methods and findings   The scope of the review covered:

1) An investigation of the costs and performance of the service compared to a 'near neighbour' with a similar environment and also other authorities who had in fact contracted their refuse collection services out.
2) An investigation of the location and viability of three depots.
3) An analysis of the department's approach to minimising the cost of purchasing consumables (eg plastic sacks).
4) A review of level of administration and supervisory support.
5) An assessment as to whether the level and scope for charges made for collection of commercial refuse and special items such as bulky refuse and garden refuse were adequate.
6) A review of the policy for the renewal of vehicles, their utilisation and their maintenance costs.

Results   After detailed negotiations between the unions involved, the management and consultants it was agreed that it would be possible to operate an effective service on only 15 rounds employing a total of about 75 men. In terms of productivity this reduction would mean that the number of premises to be covered in each weekly round would be 7,000 compared to 5,000 on the old basis. This level of productivity compared very favourably with 'contracted out' authorities. It was put to the workforce that if they accepted the new productivity 'package' the authority would not go out to tender and would give them a five year contract together with an enhanced bonus scheme.

The workforce accepted the 'package' which had a 'knock on' effect in other areas, namely:

1) A reduction of five refuse vehicles to provide an annual saving in running costs together with a 'one-off' receipt for the sale of surplus vehicles.
2) A reduction of five men in the 'reserve pool' of labour to retain the balance between the 'front line' labour force and the pool.
3) A reduction in the number of supervisors and inspectors from seven to five.

The other main findings arising from the review were that:

1) Improved vehicle scheduling and maintenance arrangements would allow a reduction of two refuse freighters and one skip emptying vehicle.
2) Centralisation of all the depot facilities on to a single depot would provide:
   (*a*) better control over the allocation of reserve labour
   (*b*) improved cover for vehicle breakdowns
   (*c*) a reduction in depot operating costs
   (*d*) improved control over stores and stock levels.
3) The introduction of a two way radio communication network between the depot and the vehicle fleet would save time currently spent by the supervisor in locating crews out on route.
4) The collection of bulky items of refuse (such as fridges and settees) although not required by statute was nonetheless being

provided as a free service at a cost of about £45,000 per year. It was considered that the service should either be discontinued or become the subject of a reasonable charge.

5) A more flexible pricing policy should be introduced to achieve a more realistic balance between the larger and small commercial customers. It was considered that adherence to an over rigid pricing policy would lead to a loss of the larger units to private operations and the levying of a rate of charge to small units that was not economic.

When the new productivity 'package' was introduced it was possible to make an annual savings on the refuse collection service as follows:

Reduced manning levels	208,000
Reduced vehicle fleet	136,000
Supervision costs	22,000
Depot costs	25,000
Annual saving	£391,000

Management are satisfied that the operation is now as lean as possible, consistent with maintaining an efficient service. The collection cost per premise now compares favourably with those of 'contracted out' authorities with the added advantage that the quality standards of the service remain firmly under the control of management.

12 Key Point Checklists for Decision Makers

The purpose of this chapter is to provide decision makers with a set of key questions which they may address to senior officers to help them evaluate the overall value for money arrangements in services for which they are responsible. Neither the questions nor the general areas for assessment selected are meant to be exhaustive. They are designed as 'test the water' questions which if not answered satisfactorily or confidently will allow the politician to make more searching enquiries perhaps through a formal review. The questioning, whether carried out informally or formally by asking officers to attend meetings of performance review committees, will enable the politician to get a 'feel' for the overall attitude towards value for money in specific departments and to find out if his officers have a good grip on economy, efficiency and effectiveness.

The questions themselves are grouped under the main areas of resource in virtually any public service undertaking, namely:

Manpower planning
Land and property
Cash and debt management
Supplies and services
Charges for services
Energy
Capital expenditure
Computers and new technology
Management services

They in turn have been selected from the 14 key areas of VFM controls identified by a Chartered Institute of Public Finance and Accountancy working party. More detailed questionnaires are available for each of these areas in the Price Waterhouse/Gee & Co 'Value for Money Auditing Manual'.

Key Review Area:
MANPOWER MANAGEMENT

KEY REVIEW ELEMENT	KEY REVIEW QUESTION
PLANNING OF MANPOWER REQUIREMENTS	How are work plans and objectives translated to manpower needs by number, type, location?
FORECASTING MANPOWER AVAILABILITY TO MEET REQUIREMENTS	Is an up to date inventory of current manpower maintained listing skills, experience, qualifications.
ACTION PLANS TO MEET MANPOWER REQUIREMENTS	What plans exist to fill gaps and deal with surpluses?
MANPOWER PLANNING SHOULD BE INTEGRATED FUNCTION	What liaison and interface exists between personnel specialists and departmental heads?
IMPLEMENTATION OF ACTION PLANS SHOULD BE MONITORED	Are manpower plans monitored and updated. Are new posts critically reviewed, by whom?
REGULAR REPORTS TO BE PREPARED ON EFFICIENCY/ PRODUCTIVITY OF MANPOWER	What performance measures are used to help adjust monitoring levels to changing work levels?

Key Review Area:
LAND AND PROPERTY

KEY REVIEW ELEMENT | KEY REVIEW QUESTION

OBJECTIVE

 To what extent do the objectives in respect of land and property interface with other policies eg: Industrial development? Are assets treated as investments and acquisitions and disposals made to achieve the greatest benefit?

ORGANISATION

 Is there a separate committee responsible for land and property holdings? Who is directly responsible for negotiating the role of surplus land and property? How are requirements assessed? Is there provision for opportunity purchases? Are objective appraisals made of proposed purchases which include running costs? What procedures are adopted to ensure that the price for surplus land is the best obtainable? What marketing methods are used (are parcels of land offered to adjoining owners)?

INFORMATION

What procedures exist for bringing surplus land and property to the notice of top management? How is the potential for letting land and property evaluated? Is the sale of land processed quickly once identified?

Key Review Area:
CASH MANAGEMENT

KEY REVIEW ELEMENT   KEY REVIEW QUESTION

CASH MANAGEMENT   Are day-to-day and period cash flow
                           forecasts prepared to monitor
                           financial performance of the
                           authority? Are all grants and
                           subsidies due to authorities
                           identified? By whom? Are prompt
                           billing procedures observed for
                           sundry debtors? Are external
                           investments or cash deposit accounts
                           regularly reviewed? Are all bankings
                           made promptly? Is value dating used?

BORROWING POLICY   Is there a one year and a three/four
                           year plan? Is the plan flexible to
                           account for sudden changes in market
                           conditions? What temporary
                           borrowing methods are used (eg call
                           money, 2 day money)?

PROFESSIONAL   To what extent are loan terms
PRACTICE   negotiated? Are administrative costs
                           for debt management kept to a
                           minimum?

INTEREST PAYMENTS   How does the average or pool rate of
                           interest compare with other
                           authorities?

Key Review Area:
SUPPLIES AND SERVICES

KEY REVIEW ELEMENT

KEY REVIEW QUESTION

STRUCTURE OF
THE SERVICE

 Is there a central purchasing unit and
if there is what are the guidelines
concerning items or services that
must be purchased centrally (eg
insurance, microcomputers)?

PURCHASING
PROCEDURES

Are there standing orders which
clearly define for example the level at
which it is necessary to go out to
tender and the minimum number of
suppliers to be circulated? Has action
been taken to aggregate departmental
requirements for similar items so that
maximum discounts can be obtained?
Is the most economic source being
used for each item?

STATISTICS AND
DOCUMENTATION

Is the paperwork system adequate for
ensuring for example the invoice
prices agree with order prices? Are
statistics available which analyse
usage by department or cost centre?

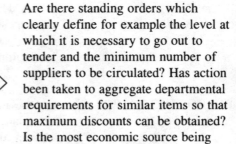

Key Review Area:
CHARGES AND SERVICES

KEY REVIEW ELEMENT

KEY REVIEW QUESTION

**REASONS FOR
CHARGE**

Is it inherently appropriate there
should be a charge for service? Is the
objective to raise income? If so, is a
target cash amount sought? Is the
maximum income possible sought?

**FIXING THE LEVEL
OF CHARGES**

Are customer/user views taken into
account? Is the ability of the customer
to pay assessed? Is elasticity of
demand taken into account? (eg
differential prices for peak or off
peak services)? What other policies
influence pricing decisions (eg
tourism, shopping car parks)? Are
comparisons made to charges by
other authorities (eg leisure centres)?
Are alternative charging systems
considered (eg membership
schemes)?

**REVIEW OF
CHARGES**

Is the review of charges made
regularly (eg annual, in-line with cost
changes)? Who reviews charges
(service committees)? How are the
effects of price changes monitored
(eg reductions in demand)?

Key Review Area:
ENERGY CONSERVATION

KEY REVIEW ELEMENT	KEY REVIEW QUESTION

CONTROL OF ENERGY

Who is responsible for energy management both centrally and at each main location? Does analysis identify relationships between consumption of energy and level of activity? Are tariffs regularly reviewed to ensure the most economical tariffs are used? Are any steps taken to smooth peaks in demand?

USES OF ENERGY

Is building insulation adequate? For what periods are buildings heated? Is heating controlled manually, by time clocks, or by thermostat? Are pipes and tanks adequately lagged?

INVESTMENT IN ENERGY CONSERVATION

Is there a training programme for all staff to conserve energy? Is there a list of energy saving investments under review, ranked in order of priority, analysed by cost and return on investment? Have specialist energy conservation officers been taken on? Do they pay their way?

Key Review Area:
CAPITAL EXPENDITURE

KEY REVIEW ELEMENT	KEY REVIEW QUESTION
APPROVALS	What officers are responsible for the approval procedure? What safeguards exist to guard against the production of abortive work?
APPRAISAL	Are all social, environmental and political factors identified? Is a multi-disciplinary approach adopted? Are realistic assessments of phased expenditure made? Is the payback method of costing used for cost saving schemes or similar methods? Are all consequences for future revenue costs identified (eg financing charges, staffing)? Are all capital costs included (eg inflation)? Are all reasonable alternative schemes properly costed?
FINAL APPROVAL	Are changes to the scheme since the initial and succeeding stages of approval identified? Prior to final approval is a re-assessment of the needs and objectives for the project made?
CONTROL OF PROJECT IMPLEMENTATION	Is a project leader nominated? Is a network analysis approach used? What is the procedure for monitoring costs against the budget? Are appropriate committees told of significant cost fluctuations and variations?
REVIEW	Is there a review procedure upon completion of a project by an independent review body?

Key Review Area:
COMPUTER SERVICES

KEY REVIEW ELEMENT	KEY REVIEW QUESTION
POSITION OF COMPUTER SERVICES WITHIN THE AUTHORITY	Is there a chief officers steering committee? Is there a computer sub-committee of politicians? Is there an established strategy for equipment acquisition and systems development?
ORGANISATION OF COMPUTER DEPARTMENT	Are the department's staffing levels in line with that required by the agreed systems development plans?
DEPARTMENTAL COSTING	Are user departments directly recharged for computer facilities?
PERSONNEL POLICIES	Are there established career paths for staff and are training programmes in existence to meet both career developments and systems plans?
CONTROL OF COMPUTER OPERATIONS	Are computer usage figures maintained? Do they analyse lost time eg systems failure?
HARDWARE AND SOFTWARE ACQUISITION	Are feasibility studies carried out for all new systems? Do they analyse costs and benefits? How is a decision made to proceed? Are detailed evaluations carried out for the acquisition of new equipment and support software? Is there a central control over the purchase of micros.

Key Review Area:
MANAGEMENT SERVICES

KEY REVIEW ELEMENT	KEY REVIEW QUESTION

**ORGANISATION
OF THE UNIT**

 To whom does the head of the unit report? Do the organisation's arrangements permit an independent and objective approach and allow ready access to senior management and politicians where appropriate? What are the overall objectives of the unit and what indicators are used to measure its success (eg savings achieved, number of reports accepted)?

WORK STUDY

 To what extent are work study officers involved in reviewing working methods and practices rather than purely work measurement and bonus scheme administration?

**ORGANISATION AND
METHODS WORK
(O & M)**

Is the content of O & M reports pitched at a reasonably high level? Is the section meant to be self financed? Is the level of experience and qualification of the staff adequate for the role demanded of them?

Bibliography

UNITED KINGDOM

Anthony, RN. 'Can Non-Profit Organisations Be Well Managed?' *vital speeches of the day* 18 February 1971.

Audit Commission for Local Authorities in England & Wales, *Improving Economy, efficiency and effectiveness in Local Government in England and Wales: An Audit Commission Handbook*, London 1983.

Chartered Institute of Public Finance and Accountancy (CIPFA). *Local Government Value for Money Handbook (Volumes 1, 2 and 3)*, London 1984.

CIPFA, *Management Guide to Contracting out in Local and Health Authorities*, London 1984.

Chapman, L. *'Your Disobedient Servant'*. Chatto and Windus, 1978.

Edmonds, J. 'The Dudley Experience': *The use of consultants in local government to promote greater economy and efficiency*, Stourbridge 1983.

Glynn, J. *Value for Money Auditing in the Public sector*. Prentice Hall, 1985.

Laing, W. *Contracting out in the National Health Service*, Public Money, December 1982.

Price Waterhouse. *Value for Money Auditing Manual*. Gee & Co, 1983.

Pryke, R. The comparative performance of public and private enterprise, *Fiscal Studies* No 3, 1982.

Redwood, J. and Hatch, J. *Controlling public industries*. Basil Blackwell, 1982.

Redwood, J. *Going for broke: gambling with taxpayers' money.* Basil Blackwell, 1984.

Savas, E.S. Comparative costs of public and private enterprise in a municipal service, in *Public and private enterprise in a mixed economy.* MacMillan, 1980.

Savas, E.S. *Privatising the Public Sector: How to shrink government.* Chatham House Publishers, 1982.

CANADA

Brown, R.E., Williams, M.C., Gallagher T.P. *Auditing Performance in government: Concepts and Cases.* Toronto and New York: John Wiley & Sons, 1982, Ronald Press, 1982.

Canadian Comprehensive Auditing Foundation. *Value for money in municipalities: A Councillor's introduction to comprehensive auditing,* 1984.

CCAF. *Value for money management. A summary of program evaluation in Canada, 1984.*

City of Thunder Bay. *Performance Measurement Manual and Catalogue.* City of Thunder Bay, 1980.

Office of the Auditor General. *An approach to comprehensive auditing,* Ottawa, 1981.

Rutman, L. *Planning useful evaluations.* Saga Library of Social Research, 1980.

Washnis, G.J. *Productivity Improvement Handbook for State and Local Government.* John Wiley, 1980.

USA

Hatry, H.P., Blair, L.H., Fisk, D.M., Greiner, J.M., Hall, J.R. and Schaeman, P.S. *How effective are your community services?* Urban Institute, Washington, 1977

Hatrty, H.P., Winnie, R.E. and Fisk, D.M. *Practical program evaluation for state and local governments.* The Urban Institute, 1981.

Sheridan, R.G. *State Budgeting in Ohio.* College of Urban Affairs, 1978.

Urban Institute, The. *Performance Measurement: a guide for local elected officers,* Washington, 1980.

Wess, K. and Hatry, H.P. *Obtaining citizen feedback. The application of citizen survey to local government.* Urban Institute, 1973.

SWEDEN
National Audit Bureau. *Performance analysis: why and how?* Stockholm: 1980.

Index